5k Training for Beginners

From Couch to 5k Runner in 8 Weeks or Less

By Jago Holmes, CPT

Updated in 2022

Disclaimer

Table Of Contents

About This Book

"The starting point of all achievement is desire. Keep this constantly in mind. Weak desires bring weak results, just as a small amount of fire makes a small amount of heat."

- Napoleon Hill

Hi there, my name is Jago Holmes, principal trainer here at New Image Personal Training in the UK.

An extremely warm welcome to my running program, **5k Training for Beginners - From Couch to 5k Runner in 8 Weeks or Less,** where you will learn all you need to know about training for and running a 5k race, from the basics at grass roots level, right through to developing an advanced understanding of how to get the best out of your training. I take you from the idea stage right through to actually running your first ever 5k.

If you've ever thought seriously about running a 5k and you've never done any running before, no doubt you'll have looked into it in some depth. Whilst running a 5k race doesn't compare to the gruelling and often unforgiving marathon distance, you'll still need a very good level of fitness.

When you've accomplished your goal you'll still feel very proud of how far you've come and what you've accomplished. Anyone you know that has ever been interested in their own health and fitness will have a good deal of respect for you because you have followed through on your goal and the fact that you didn't just dream it, you actually went out and did it!

Every journey, whether long or short, starts with just one small step. Your first step has been to get hold of this training guide.

Inside you will find out absolutely everything you need to know about running a 5k race. I take you from a complete beginner with little or no fitness, through to achieving a good level of fitness (much fitter than the average person on the street), all the way through to running your first 5k.

I look at all the aspects of running, from choosing the right training gear, getting started, understanding how your body needs to be encouraged to change, avoiding injuries, and the quickest ways of improving your fitness and endurance, right the way through to race day and beyond. I also provide four different training programs based on varying levels of starting fitness, so you can tailor this training to your need.

By the time you have read this guide you'll not only understand exactly what it takes to run a 5k, but also by following one of the unique programs I have designed for you, you will have all the tools needed to be able to actually physically run one.

My advice for complete beginners is to **allow at least 6 – 8 weeks to reach the required level of fitness,** or longer if you can't be consistent. This is how I have structured this system. Obviously, you will have busy weeks, get sick or possibly injured at times, which may all force you to miss some training. But if you maintain consistency as much as possible, you will be ready in this amount of time.

I always recommend actually booking your place on a race in advance so that you have made a psychological and physical commitment to your goal. Once you have made this type of commitment to something it is far more unlikely that you will back out.

One last point before you start reading: beware of the old saying, "if a little is good a lot is better." More is definitely not always better in relation to your training as a beginner. With an increase in physical activity comes increased risk of injury and burnout. The best advice is to proceed slowly and gradually increase the frequency, duration and intensity of the activities with planned rest periods. In the programs I've designed for you, you'll see these principles strongly adhered to.

Anyway, make yourself a drink, sit down and get comfortable and start reading. The quicker you understand what you need to do, then the faster you will be able to get started.

Good luck! – Jago

Section 1 – The Theory

What Is a 5k Race?

*"I think there is something, more important than believing: Action!
The world is full of dreamers, there aren't enough who will move
ahead and begin to take concrete steps to actualize their vision."*
- W. Clement Stone

A 5k race is essentially a race set over 5 kilometres (3.1 miles) which
will take the average person between 30 – 60 minutes to complete.
The fastest ever time for a man completing a 5k was 12 minutes 37
seconds, which was accomplished in 2004 by the Ethiopian distance
runner Kenenisa Bekele. The fastest women's time was 14 minutes
11 seconds, which was set by Tirunesh Dibaba in Oslo in 2008.

The 5k race is the most popular distance run with thousands of
events set up all year round all over the world. The comparatively
short distance means it has an appeal to most people who would
like to start running and need a focus and a target to aim for.

Some of the most popular races have tens of thousands of
participants of all ages and from all walks of life. 5k races tend to
lend themselves very well to fun runs and fundraising events
because of the shorter and more achievable distance compared to
the other traditional races, such as 10k, half marathons and full
marathons. These all require a much higher level of commitment
and determination to be able to run.

Many charities raise very large amounts of money from participants
who choose to represent their cause. Getting sponsorship from
people you know before you run the race is another great idea
because it ties you in to your goal a little more and will focus your

mind during your training when you feel less than motivated to get out and run.

Starting Out

Whenever a building is being built, its strength and longevity will be determined by creating strong and effective foundations. So too is the case with your own fitness. Getting this part right can really make the rest of your training much easier, allowing you to progress much faster.

First things first: go to your doctor for a check up and get any niggles or injuries looked at by a physiotherapist. Don't begin if any old injuries still cause you pain as they may develop into serious long-term problems and hamper your progress.

● Write down your goals and break them in to smaller and more manageable chunks.
● Plan your routes using the programs in this manual.
● Assess your running style (gait) so you can buy an effective and comfortable pair or pairs of running shoes.
● Get any other clothing that you might need such as gloves, hats and waterproofs for winter training and a couple of pairs of specialist running socks.

If you are a beginner and new to running, select the program that you feel is most suitable for you and start at the beginning.

There are two main considerations regarding running a 5k race. Firstly, the 3.1 miles you will be running needs to be respected. The majority of people off the street couldn't simply nip out and run that distance without any practice. Secondly, such a task requires adequate preparation and training and you must ask yourself if you possess the discipline and desire to complete the necessary training for the event.

If the answer is yes, then you are good to go!

Setting Goals to Get What You Want

"Goals are a means to an end, not the ultimate purpose of our lives. They are simply a tool to concentrate our focus and move us in a direction. The only reason we really pursue goals is to cause ourselves to expand and grow. Achieving goals by themselves will never make us happy in the long term; it's who you become, as you overcome the obstacles necessary to achieve your goals, that can give you the deepest and most long-lasting sense of fulfilment."

- Anthony Robbins

Every journey starts with just one small step. It is how you go about taking that step that is the important part. Goals give us a direction to head out in and take action. One of the most important steps in this process is to actually write your goals down. Your brain needs targets to aim for; that is how we are conditioned.

Most people simply have vague dreams and desires that they will probably never achieve. If we don't set definite goals we will simply end up in a place dictated to us by chance. A goal that excites, challenges or inspires you is one that you are most likely to go on to achieve.

Running a 5k race is a great goal to have, but it is a challenge nevertheless, something that requires more than a little haphazard training. You will need to be determined as well as physically fit. Setting yourself some structured short- and long-term goals will help you to get through your preparation.

It is important to get emotionally connected to the feelings that achieving your goal will give you, such as a feeling of success or accomplishment. We need to program our subconscious mind to strive towards achieving this goal. By giving your goals emotional triggers that we associate pain or unhappiness with, we can do this. The truth is that most people give more thought to planning their holidays or a dinner party than they do to planning the things that they want to achieve in life. Thoughts and goals are your starting point.

There are two basic types of goals, process goals and outcome goals. It is important to set short-term objectives (process goals) on your way to achieving the big goal (outcome goal). The definitions and examples of process and outcome goals are listed below:

Process Goals

These types of goals involve activities that help to improve your ability to achieve your outcome goals. Examples of process goals include:

- I will follow this training program closely
- I will change my diet and only eat treat foods once a week
- I will try to sleep at least 8 hours every night, etc.

Outcome Goals

These goals relate to the finished product or end goal.

For example, for your first 5k race you might decide that the following goals are very appropriate:

- I have managed to run the whole 3.1 miles
- I have just completed my first ever 5k in under 35 minutes
- I was able to run the second half of the race faster than the first

Your next task is to sit down and make a list of all the things that you would like to accomplish through your training. Don't worry about whether they make any sense or not or are achievable at this stage, simply get your thoughts down on paper. When you have done this, the next step is to make sure they are SMART. I'll tell you about this in a minute.

There may be times during your training when you will question your reasons for putting yourself through this challenge and times when you will feel that you are not making progress. By working through and checking off your list of short- and long-term goals, you will be able to justify the progress you are making.

The key to setting goals is to use the **S.M.A.R.T.** acronym. The meaning of this is as follows:

S is for SPECIFIC

Make your goals specific to what you want to achieve and the actions you will be taking that will allow you to reach those goals. If you are training to run a 5k race, for example, and your training is based solely around that factor, then setting the goal of being able to row 1,000 meters in under 4 minutes is not really relevant. All fitness is specific. Just because you are fitter in one type of discipline, let's say swimming, doesn't mean you'll automatically be good at cycling.

M is for MEASURABLE

A measurable goal is one that you can physically measure. Having a goal that states that you would like to feel better isn't measurable at all. However, if you take that same goal and rate yourself before you start on a scale of wellness from one to ten (let's say you feel like a five out of ten) and then you set a goal of feeling seven out of ten in six weeks' time, then you have a much more measurable goal.

Running is ideal for setting measurable goals. "I ran one mile without stopping" or "I ran the whole of my new running route: are examples of specific and measurable goals.

A is for ACHIEVEABLE

It is a very important part of the equation to ensure that the goals you set yourself are achievable. It can be a very demotivating process if the goals you set are too high. You will never have the satisfaction of achieving them and ticking them off your list. The satisfaction of moving forwards is boosted by achieving your goals along the way.

R is for REALISTIC

Realistic goals have the end target in mind but are also realistic in their expectations. For example, if you are a beginner and one of your aims is to be able to run a 5k race, it would be a realistic goal to be able to do this within 6 – 8 weeks, whereas doing this within just 2 weeks is completely unrealistic.

T is for TIME-FRAMED

A time-framed goal has a specific date or length of time that you will set yourself in order to be able to achieve it. For example, "I want to be able to run 2 miles without stopping in 3 weeks' time" would be a specifically time-framed goal.

A very important part of setting your goals is to write them in the present tense so they become more realistic in your own mind. They have a much more powerful effect written in this way. By writing goals like this it is almost as though you are just recording what you have already achieved.

Here is an example of two goals. The second one is written in present tense.

"I would like to be able to run a 5k race in 6 weeks' time."

"I have just completed my first ever 5k race. It has taken me just 6 weeks to train for it and I feel wonderfully elated about what I have achieved."

Which of these two examples do you think will have a more powerful effect? Which would you feel the most satisfaction and motivation from reading?

Another way to formalize a goal is to commit yourself financially to one. For example, once you have decided on a race/date, you could register for the event and make hotel reservations or book train tickets, etc., if necessary. By committing yourself financially to your goals, you are more likely to keep on track during the harder times of your training program.

One final but very important point you need to consider when setting goals is that they should be broken down into smaller chunks. Here are some SMART 6-week goals:

"I have registered for a 5k race."
"I have bought a new pair of running shoes specifically for my running style."
"I can run 3 miles without having to stop."
"I have been running 3 times a week, every week."

Good examples of long-term goals would be:

"I completed the New York Marathon on dd/mm/yyyy. It was a great feeling finally realizing my goal after 6 months of training."

"Combined with my training and changes to my diet, I have lost 1 stone for my wedding anniversary on dd/mm/yyyy."

Tracking Your Progress

"It is important that you recognize your progress and take pride in your accomplishments. Share your achievements with others. Brag a little. The recognition and support of those around you is nurturing."

- Rosemarie Rossetti

Another tool that you can use that goes hand in hand with your goal setting notes is to keep a training log.

It doesn't matter what you use to chart your progress, a diary, notebook, computer spread sheet, anything, just do it. Keep notes and record all the details about your training.

Some of the things you need to record are as follows:

- The date and time of day you do your training runs.
- The distance or time that you ran during that session.
- How you felt both physically and mentally before, during, and after the run.
- You could also record your resting heart rate before you started and again straight afterwards.

If you use the same route over 2 or 3 different occasions and aim to complete it in about the same time, take your heart rate immediately after finishing the run. As you get more fit, you will in theory place less demand on your heart, therefore your heart rate should be slower (fewer beats per minute) on subsequent runs.

If you really want to go in to detail, you may want to include things like:

- The weather

- The route you took
- What you wore
- Whether you felt any aches or pains
- Your pre-training meal

If you wear a heart-rate monitor, record your average and max heart rate for your run.

There are a number of benefits to recording your workouts, but perhaps the most relevant one is to chart your progress. Seeing how far you've come from your earlier workouts can really highlight the progress you have made so far, giving you a boost, especially on your down days.

Also, making a note of any aches and pains early on may help to prevent them developing into much more serious, longer-term problems.

Keeping track of your mileage is also a good idea for two main reasons. Primarily, it will help to chart your progress towards your goals, but also it will help to keep an eye on the amount of wear you are giving your running shoes. You'll know when it is time to get a new pair when you've run around the 350 – 400-mile mark.

I really do recommend at least keeping the bare minimum of details about your training, but the more information you can record the better it will be to chart your progress and keep a check on injuries and niggles, etc. You will also find that committing these details to paper means that you are increasing the importance of this task in your life and programming your subconscious mind towards success.

Checking the Way You Run

"Running gait" is basically a term used to describe the way a person runs. One of the first considerations for every serious runner should be what type of footwear is most appropriate for your particular running style or gait. By choosing the right training shoes you can avoid placing a strain on the muscles and joints of the body which are subjected to constant impact over the course of a training session. Assessing your running style is important so you can understand your own type of gait.

We use the term "pronation" to analyze gait, which is basically the lower legs' natural way of absorbing shock. It is the movement of the foot from heel strike to big toe push-off or to put it simply, the amount of rolling your foot does towards the inside or instep of the foot.

There are three ways that you can learn how your foot lands and leaves the floor:

#1 Look at Your Shoes

Firstly, you can take a look at the soles of the shoes you wear most often. If most of the wear is on the outside or outstep of the sole, you generally tend to under-pronate, but if the wear is more towards the inside or the instep of the sole, you are probably an over-pronator. If the wear appears evenly distributed over the sole then the chances are you have a 'neutral' running gait.

#2 The Wet Foot Test

Secondly, do the "wet foot" test. To do this, simply wet the soul of your bare foot and walk on something that will clearly show a footmark. Some colored paper, a tiled floor, or even floorboards should be able to leave a mark which you can examine to see how your foot lands.

#3 The Treadmill Test

Specialized running analysis equipment can also be used to find your running gait. This is probably the most reliable and accurate indicator. Most good running stores now have this technology free for you to use. During the test, your footprint is checked using a treadmill or a sensored pad. The tester can then see where the foot impact is the greatest and accurately predict your type of pronation.

There are 3 levels of pronation:

Under-pronation (supination)

If you are an **under-pronator** you will be in the minority, as this is the least common type of running gait. This style involves pushing off from the outside of the foot and will require more support on the outside of your shoes.

Neutral-pronation

This is the most desirable type of pronation, where the foot plant lands on the outside of the heel and rolls inward slightly to absorb shock whilst moving off the big toe.

Over-pronation

This is the most common type of running gait. It is estimated that nearly 70% of all runners have this style. If you over-pronate, your foot will land on the outer edge of the heel which flattens the arch as the foot strikes the ground. As the footstep progresses to push-off it rolls excessively towards the instep, and you will therefore require support on the inside or instep of the shoe

For most people this isn't a problem as the distances run aren't too challenging. But when the length of run begins to increase, there is a real risk of injury, so check that your shoes are designed for this type of running style. If poor gait habits develop, this action can lead to foot pain as well as knee pain, shin splints, Achilles tendinitis, posterior tibial tendinitis, and plantar fasciitis.

Out of the following examples using the "wet foot test," you can see whether you have sunken (low) arches, neutral arches, or raised arches which all indicate a certain type of foot pronation.

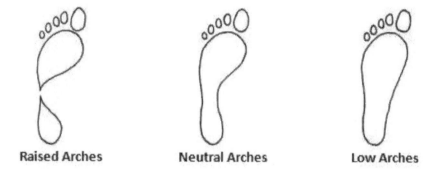

Raised Arches   **Neutral Arches**   **Low Arches**

Raised arches – Indicates that your feet under-pronate when running.

If your footprint looks like this, you are an under-pronator and have a high-arched foot. Your footprint will leave a very thin band, or none at all, on the lateral side (outside of the foot) between the heel and forefoot. This is because most under-pronators are forefoot runners, only using the heel downhill. This curved, highly-arched foot does not pronate sufficiently and requires a lot of cushioning.

Neutral arches – This footfall is ideal for running.

If your print looks like this, you have a normal foot plant and are a neutral runner. A normal foot usually leaves approximately half the footprint - the lateral (outside) part.

Low arches – Indicates over-pronation because there is only a small amount of support stopping your foot rolling inwards.

If your print looks like this and your foot leaves a print of the whole of the foot, you have a flatter foot because the arch collapses through the foot motion. The foot strikes at the heel and rolls inwards excessively - this is over-pronation. If you are a serious over-pronator and do not wear the correct shoes, then you are much more likely to suffer from injuries (especially knee and hip injuries) when running.

Choosing Your Running Equipment

"If you believe you can, you probably can. If you believe you won't, you most assuredly won't. Belief is the ignition switch that gets you off the launching pad."

- Denis Waitley

How Should I Select My Running Shoes?

There is no such thing as the best running shoe in the world, because everyone is different and everyone has different attributes and requirements as a runner. Unsurprisingly, there are too many individual variables to make the perfect shoe for everyone. Key factors affecting your choice of running shoe typically include different biomechanics (your gait), different body weight, shape of foot, width of foot, the surfaces you run on, and how often you run.

Getting the correct fit is the most important part of the equation when choosing your footwear and clothing. This is not only to achieve maximum performance, but also to avoid blistering and more serious injuries.

Obviously, the main consideration when choosing running shoes is to select a pair that is designed with your running gait in mind.

Running shoes are usually split in to three basic categories – cushioned, support, and control.

Cushioned shoes

These shoes are for under-pronators. Runners requiring cushioned shoes often run on their toes and have a raised arch. These running shoes provide little stability but are softer underfoot and more cushioned.

Support shoes

Suitable for neutral runners, support shoes are usually best for runners with a 'regular' or neutral foot plant. Support shoes usually combine good cushioning with lightweight support features on the medial (inner) side of the shoe in order to limit excessive inward rolling of the foot.

Control shoes

These are best for more serious over-pronators and also for heavier runners. Serious over-pronators usually have a flatter foot as their arch collapses through the foot strike. These shoes are generally heavier and combine cushioning with extra support to provide essential protection which reduces the risk of injury.

Do I Need New Shoes?

The most important investment you can make to help you run is buying one or two pairs of decent running shoes. If you already have some running shoes, make sure that they are not too old and have plenty of cushioning still present in the sole, which helps to maximize the absorption of the impact of your stride.

Analyze the need to purchase running shoes based on the number of miles your old pair has been run in or their age. Don't base your decision on the need for new shoes by just looking at the soles for the remaining tread they have.

The mid-sole of many running shoes breaks down at 350 - 400 miles (or earlier depending on a number of factors) and offers little or no protection after that period of time. It is important to keep in mind that running shoes provide the first line of defense against potential injury.

A good idea is to buy two pairs of the same running shoes and then alternate their use each training day. This increases the life expectancy of each pair.

If you do need to purchase a new pair of shoes that you expect to wear during the race, make sure that you do so at least 4 – 6 weeks prior. These shoes should be the same type that you've found to work well for you during your long runs. The key point here is to have sufficient time to break the new pair in (by logging 60-70 miles including one long run) prior to your race.

There are many different styles to choose from when selecting a running shoe, and the proper choice depends on a few factors. Try not to get too hung up on the color or the appearance of the shoes, but make sure you are choosing the right kind for your feet and body type.

Visit a specialist running shop to get a free expert assessment. They will be able to advise you as to which type of shoe suits your particular running style. (See the section on running gait for more details.)

Try on shoes later in the day when your feet have swollen to their full size. Take the socks you normally run with you to the shoe store.

The shoes need to mould to the shape of your feet, so they should be a snug fit at the sides and across the top. Good running shoes tend to be as lightweight as possible while at the same time offering the maximum amount of support for your foot and gait type.

But there are also some other factors that need to be considered when choosing running shoes:

Your shoe size – Make sure the shoe you select fits properly, with no movement or slippage at the heel. Check that your toes are not crushed into the toe box at the front of the shoe. Bear in mind that the foot will expand when running longer distances, so you might need a shoe size a little bigger. The usual recommendation is to allow half an inch or a thumb's width of room from the front of your running shoe to the end of the longest toe. The reason for this is that the foot expands when running long distances (i.e. anything over a couple of miles) and this extra room in the toe box helps avoid painful sore toes and nasty black toenails.

How much you weigh - When you run, up to 2-3 times your body weight is forced down onto your running shoes. The heavier you are, the more support, cushioning, and stability you will need.

The surface you run on - Your shoe requires the correct sole type for your needs. Road shoes have a shallow, hard-wearing tread. On-and-off-road shoes require a tread with deep enough lugs for grip whilst being durable enough not to wear out on roads.

Broad or narrow foot - Simply put, shoes that fit better will perform better. Although most brands are built on a standard D-width fitting, some are broader and some narrower than normal.

Man or woman - If you're a woman, buy shoes designed for women. If you're a man, buy shoes designed for men. Men and women's feet vary in shape and size, so it's essential to make sure that you buy a shoe specific to your gender. Women's feet are narrower, particularly around the heel, and men's feet tend to be broader.

Care of Your Running Shoes

- Wear your running shoes *only* for running. They will last much longer by doing this.
- Do not machine wash or tumble dry your running shoes. If your shoes become dirty, hand wash them with commercial shoe care products.
- When your running shoes become wet, stick bundled-up newspaper inside to accelerate the drying time and help them to keep their shape.

Training Gear

The selection of appropriate clothing and footwear is vital to your comfort when running long distances, as the constant rubbing of material against skin can be very uncomfortable after a while.

Here are my recommendations for training gear:

Socks

These are a very important factor to consider as your feet will be subjected to constant movement, friction, and rubbing. You should buy a couple of good-quality, specialized running socks or synthetic blend socks which will wick sweat away from the skin and allow your feet to breathe.

Shorts and Trousers

Again, select shorts and trousers that wick away sweat, reduce chafing, and allow your skin to breathe. The general rule of thumb here (although not always true) is the more you spend, the higher-quality comfort you will have.

Running Tops

Tops need to be breathable, comfortable, and not rub or irritate the skin. In colder weather and in windy conditions, you should consider wearing an old t-shirt that you can discard once your long run or race begins, but be sure that you won't be running into the wind later on your return route. Alternatively, you could wear another lightweight top and then tie this around your waist when you heat up.

If you decide to wear a hat, it will trap body heat. This is great in cold weather, but a bad idea for running in hot and humid conditions.

Do not over-dress. You should assess the need to wear tights, long-sleeves, gloves, etc., as excess clothing can lead to the body overheating. Doing so can make the "real feel" 10 degrees warmer once you begin running.

If you are training in the winter, though, it is important to wrap up. Although running will keep you warm to some degree, when running outside for hours in the cold your body temperature may start to drop because of a redistribution of blood to the working muscles. This will affect your extremities because of reduced blood flow, something you will feel particularly in your hands, feet, and head.

Sports Bra

An often-neglected item of clothing for women is the selection of an appropriate sports bra. You should select a sports bra that is a good fit, but also one that is geared to give you maximum support for long-distance running. It is best to buy your bra from a sports shop rather than a clothing shop.

Here are some tips for choosing the right sports bra:

- Measure around your body under the bust to give the size of the bra - you measure here because the flesh of the rib cage is firm and a snugly fitted under band is the key to making you feel supported.
- Once you have your under-bust measurement, you will be able to assess your cup size.
- Before choosing a sports bra, take into account the requirements of your particular sporting activity. This, coupled with your cup size, will determine the level of support you need.
- If your bra pulls up at the back, it is too big in the under band around the belly.
- If there is any extra space under the cup or loose fabric around the nipple, then the bra cup size is too big.
- When the bra you have chosen is too small you will usually notice flesh poking out towards the armpit and above the cup
- If your bra is making a mark and cutting in around your shoulders or body then it is too small.

Fact or Fiction

Fact: Female breasts are primarily composed of glandular tissue and fat and are held in position by delicate ligaments.

Fact: There are no muscles in the breast.

Fiction: Some exercises can return your breasts to their original shape.

Fact: Once breasts have dropped because of stretched ligaments, **NOTHING** can restore them to their former position.

Often people underestimate the importance of good training kit and how it will affect your run and limit your chances of injury and levels of discomfort.

Within reason, train at least a few times in what you will wear on the day of the event so you can test your outfit for comfort and practicality. As you get closer to race day, change as little of your training equipment as possible. You don't want to be breaking in new shoes on the day, as the changes to your foot position could very well have disastrous consequences.

Running Gadgets and Performance Enhancers

"Every single life only becomes great when the individual sets upon a goal or goals which they really believe in, which they can really commit themselves to, which they can put their whole heart and soul into."

- Brian Tracy

As time progresses, the technology we have at our fingertips also improves. Over the last few years there have been some very important developments in the area of tracking and monitoring the way we run, how far we run, and how fast. Here is a summary of a few of these with my recommendations for what you may find useful.

Pedometer

The humble pedometer now seems like a very basic type of instrument, but it can still deliver some very useful information.

A pedometer or step counter is a portable device that counts each step a person takes by detecting the movement of their hips. Because the distance of each person's step varies, an individual calibration needs to be done by the user before using if a standardized distance (such as kilometers or miles) is needed.

Pedometers are very useful in providing motivation and statistics for anyone wanting to become more active in everyday life. They are usually worn on a belt or waistband and used to record how many steps the wearer has walked or run, and thus the kilometers/miles (distance = number of steps x step length) can also be calculated.

Step counters are also being integrated into an increasing number of portable electronic devices such as mp3 players and mobile phones, which use shoe sensors that transmit information to a wireless receiver. Workout information such as elapsed time, distance travelled, and calories burned can all be recorded.

Unfortunately, some basic pedometers accidentally record movements other than walking, such as bending over to tie a shoelace, or bumps from the road when travelling in a car or bus etc. The more advanced and expensive versions record fewer of these "false steps."

Another criticism of the standard pedometer is that it cannot record intensity, but this can be worked around by setting step targets within a certain time goal (for example, 1000 steps in a certain amount of time).

Heart Rate Monitor

A heart rate monitor is a monitoring tool that allows you to measure your heart rate and, if you wish, record it for later evaluation.

These usually consist of two parts: a chest transmitter attached by an adjustable fabric strap, and a wrist receiver, mobile phone, or other device.

Advanced versions can also measure variances in your heart rate and breathing rate to assess and monitor your level of fitness.

When a heartbeat is detected, a radio or digital signal is transmitted, which the receiver picks up to record the current heart rate. This signal can be a simple radio pulse or a unique coded signal from the chest strap.

Many heart rate monitors are also capable of giving you the following information:

- Average heart rate over exercise period
- Time spent working in a specific heart rate zone
- Calories burned over the course of the run
- Breathing rate
- Distance covered (using GPS tracking)
- Average speed (using GPS tracking)

All the above information can also be downloaded to a computer, depending on which version of heart rate monitor you buy.

Stopwatch

A stopwatch is a handheld device designed to measure the amount of time elapsed from a particular point when started to the point when the timer is stopped.

A typical stopwatch works the following way. The timing functions are traditionally controlled by two buttons on the casing. Pressing one button starts the timer running, and pressing the button a second time stops it, leaving the elapsed time displayed. A press of another button then resets the stopwatch to zero.

The second button can often be used to record split times or lap times. When the split time button is pressed while the watch is running, the display freezes, allowing the elapsed time to that point to be read, but the watch mechanism continues running to record total elapsed time. Pressing the split button a second time allows the watch to resume display of total time elapsed.

Digital stopwatches often include date and time-of-day functions as well.

The stopwatch function is usually a feature of many wrist watches and mobile phones and other portable music devices, so it is worth checking to see if you have any of these before deciding to buy one.

Marathon finishing lines use a larger digital version of a stopwatch designed for viewing at a distance called a stop clock.

GPS Running Technology

The Global Positioning System (GPS) is basically a navigational satellite system developed by the United States Department of Defense for their own air force. It is the only fully functional system that can be used freely, and can be used by individuals to track journeys and distances both on and off road all over the world.

The system relies on using between 24 and 32 satellites to transmit precise radio wave signals, which allow GPS receivers to determine their current location, time, and speed.

GPS systems adapted for running are excellent tools for calculating and tracking your own training and progress. However, before you choose a GPS watch, phone, or other device, it is important to understand how it can be used to improve your training.

There are several methods for utilizing a GPS system when running which will increase your workout productivity.

One method is simply to set a distance goal each time you run and use your GPS device to record this. For example, "Today I will run 3 miles."

Positional tracking (for tracking your location) can also be very helpful if you are doing long distances so you don't get lost, a long way from home.

Speed-based goals are another way that GPS watches and phones are useful. Rather than just tracking the distance you are running, you can focus on the pace at which you are travelling these distances.

Your GPS device has to know exactly where each satellite is in space. It calculates this from a set of orbital elements, which is simply a collection of numbers that accurately describes the satellite's orbit.

With any good GPS system you can normally expect accuracy to be within a few feet. However, the satellite signals are not able to pass through structures, so if you are out of the direct view of a satellite you probably won't get an accurate signal, or you may get one possibly reflected off another structure nearby. In this case the signal will have travelled further, so your calculated position could be incorrect. This is called "a multipath error." It's a very common problem in built-up areas such as towns and cities.

Areas that have poor reception, overhead trees, foliage, and weather conditions such as clouds, rain, snow, etc., can also have an impact on the signals you receive. These conditions can weaken signals to the point where they are unusable.

Generally speaking, you can expect newer models to be more reliable and sensitive than older ones.

Running Watch

A running watch is a very handy training aid to have. The good news is that most of the models are surprisingly easy to use, with prompts onscreen telling you which mode you have entered and what happens if you hold down a particular key.

There are some basic requirements you will need to consider before making a purchase, such as:

Is the screen readable at arm's length?
Are the buttons easy to use whilst running?

You'll find that a specialist running watch is far more than just for checking the time. It also offers users a variety of training options. Of course, if your running watch includes GPS then it will likely have many more options.

A good training watch with GPS offers many excellent features. It can act as a stopwatch and help you to track where you are or find your way to where you are going. Some running watches have even more features, such as heart rate monitors and calorie counters as well as some of the following features:

Countdown timer - Many running watches also have countdown timers. These aren't essential, but a good one can help a great deal when you're doing repetitions.

Stopwatch mode – The stopwatch mode times your runs in hours, minutes, seconds, and fractions of a second. Many models have both a start/stop button and a lap button which pauses the display without stopping the stopwatch, so you can check your time at given points such as every mile or the end of part of your training route.

Memory – Many watches can keep a record of your lap times and splits (different periods of time or distance), for example, 1-mile splits. When you enter the memory recall mode, each workout has a page showing the date and overall time of the session. You are then able to select which session you want to view and scroll through lap by lap or split by split. Some watches can also highlight the session's best lap and calculate your average lap time. Once you've finished viewing, you can choose whether to delete the session from the memory or keep it for future reference.

If you don't want all the extras that a GPS watch provides, something like one from the Garmin Forerunner range is well worth considering. You can use it for tracking your steps either for running or generally during the day. It also monitors your heart both when you're running and at rest to give you an accurate overview, and if you love music, you can choose from 1,000 songs! Some models also have detailed colored maps for planning new running routes.

Points to look consider when buying a watch
- The weight of the watch. This is usually 32 – 50 grams for comfort.
- Does the watch have a large clear dial for viewing when running?
- Does it have a long battery life and a rechargeable battery?

All these gadgets are simply tools that allow you to get more information about how you're progressing, which is a very important factor. When you're training hard and regularly, it's important to know exactly how far you've come and how far you still have to go.

By no means is any of this tech necessary for you to become a better runner or to complete any of the plans in this book for that matter; however, it's there if you choose to use it.

My advice is to buy a good device that has a heart rate monitor which also includes GPS tracking features. This way you have access to all the information you need: your heart rates, distances, speed, and times.

Mobile Phone

I would always advise any runner to carry a mobile phone for your own health, safety, and well-being. For example, you may witness an accident or incident or be involved in one yourself, get lost, or suffer an injury which renders you incapable of getting home. It's always useful to have a way of contacting someone when you are out running, just in case.

Running Apps

There is a wide range of running apps available for both iOS and Android devices; so wide, in fact, it can be a little overwhelming. It's worth spending time to find the one that suits you best; for example, you can get apps that are specifically for beginners or advanced runners and these apps help you to successfully build up your training and to hit your targets and achieve your goals. Most apps will connect to your running watch or fitness tracker.

Running apps are ideal for runners whether you are new to the sport or an experienced runner. You can use a running app to record your runs and the progress you're making and to set yourself goals and targets.

Depending on which one you use, apps can track health and performance like distance, pace, heart rate, and calories. Some apps are programmed with different training runs and routes using GPS, and some are suitable for all levels. The prices range as well; some are free to download, and others require a subscription which gives you direct access to premium features. Some apps also integrate social and competitive elements, which can be great if you like a challenge.

If you're looking for an app that will work with your Smartphone and will collect running data, Strava, Map My Run, and Runkeeper are all good choices. Strava can also be used to track swimming, cycling and workouts too. There is a free version of Strava available which makes it a good starting point and it comes with "Beacon," a feature that sends out your live location as you run, allowing family or friends to track you and helping you to stay safe as you train.

Other Great Accessories On the Market

Many runners love accessories to make their runs more pleasurable and comfortable. New brands and model updates regularly appear on the market.

Top of the list is obviously a pair of comfortable running shoes which we cover in more detail in another section, and a close second is a running belt with adequate room for storing keys, phone, credit card etc.

Compact, durable wireless headphones are ideal to enjoy music along the way, and ear buds are also very popular – but for comfort it's worth investing in some that have been designed for runners. Also, don't forget to check that they're compatible with your chosen running app.

Other products relatively new to the market are knuckle lights. These highly efficient lights are worn on the outside of your hands and offer great visibility if you want to run either early in the morning or after sunset.

Don't forget to invest in a hi-vis top and/or cap for safety so that you can be clearly seen by car users, cyclists and pedestrians.

Should You Wear Headphones?

You're going to be spending quite a bit of time on your own over the next few weeks as you train. Some people like the quiet, solitary zone of a good run, whilst others get a little bored.

Some of this time you'll be able to train with a friend, which is great for both the company and the motivation, but other times you'll have to run on your own.

Now, if you've decided to do most of your preparation on a treadmill then you'll have no problem, you can listen to music or even watch TV.

However, if you're doing most of your running outside, then at times it can a little boring and uninspiring.

Bear in mind that towards the end of your training for a half marathon, you'll be clocking up a fair few miles and your own thoughts and company might get a little tiresome.

The obvious option is to wear headphones and listen to music. There are pros and cons about this.

Pros:

- You stave some off some of the boredom of running alone.

- You get to listen to your own selection of music which can keep you entertained.

- You can carefully format the tracks so that you get a new bouncy or motivational song or
- message every few minutes.

- You can download specially designed apps for runners that include lively tracks and motivational comments to keep you focused.

- It can take your mind of any discomfort you're feeling throughout your run.

Cons

You've removed one of your main senses: your ears. This puts you at greater risk for a number of reasons.

- Other road users, especially cars during the day. At night you'll be able to see the headlights and then you'll be aware of them approaching. During the day, however, you don't have this option.

- The music can take you into an almost subconscious state where you aren't fully aware or focused on the things happening around you.

- You'll be less aware of the people you encounter and may not pick up any vibes as to whether that person could be a threat to you.

- You won't hear hazard warning signals, sirens, or car horns which can alert you to any potential dangers.

- You won't be aware of any barking dogs or other wildlife which may also pose a threat to you.

- If you're running in unfamiliar places, your ears provide another essential monitoring and navigational tool, without which you increase your chances of getting lost.

So when you're training, it may seem like an obvious option to listen to your headphones, but there are a number of things to be mindful of. If you run in very quiet rural areas then this may not be of as much concern as running in a city, but you still need to maintain your awareness at all times.

Perhaps the easiest compromise is to have your music on quietly most of the time. Then, when you know there's nothing around you and you perceive no threat (for example, while you're running around a sports field) then crank up the volume.

Just be aware that you need to keep your wits about you if you're running the streets as there are many potential threats to your safety.

How Your Body Reacts to Running

"Don't limit yourself. Many people limit themselves to what they think they can do. You can go as far as your mind lets you. What you believe, remember, you can achieve."

- Mary Kay Ash

Okay, here we go: this is the technical part which I feel must be included in any guide that promises to teach you how to run a 5k race. Don't switch off and move on to another section if you find some of it a little bit hard going. I have tried to simplify things as much as I can, but I have also included an easy-to-understand summary at the end of each section which doesn't give as much detail but gives you the main ideas.

You know your body, you know its aches and pains, twinges, and limitations, you know when you are feeling tired and lethargic and when you feel great, but there are many things about your body you can't be sure of. The strength of your heart, the pressure in your arteries, the condition of your internal organs. Only an expert will be able to tell you what sort of condition you are in internally.

It is for this reason that you should get yourself checked over by a health professional before you begin your training. What they will discover will not necessarily tell you everything, but listening to your heart, taking your blood pressure, and discussing the health history of yourself and your family may unearth something that needs to be acted upon.

Everyone will respond completely differently to running. Some will rapidly progress without injuries of any kind, whilst others really struggle to get going and pick up niggle after niggle. Everyone is different, but certain parts of all bodies work in basically the same way. That is what this section is all about.

This section will give insight into exactly how the human body responds and changes during endurance training.

The Circulatory System

The circulatory system is made up of three main elements, each with its own job to do. They are the heart, blood, and blood vessels. Here is the task each one does:

The Heart

The heart is basically a pump that supplies blood to every single part of your body. From our particular point of view the heart pumps blood to the muscles; the more you work your muscles, the greater the challenge you place them under, either by running uphill or running faster. The harder you work, the harder your heart works.

Basically, muscles need oxygenated blood in order to be able to contract and this is what the heart attempts to provide. The heart is itself a muscle and can be trained and improved like any other muscle. It can become bigger and stronger and can pump more blood around the body with every heartbeat. The amount of blood it can move with every beat is called the stroke volume. As you get fitter, the amount of oxygenated blood needed by the working muscles doesn't decrease. What changes is your heart becomes stronger and capable of pumping more blood per heartbeat, therefore increasing stroke volume.

This is the reason that beginners' heart rates are always much higher than intermediate runners, their hearts aren't as strong or efficient and they haven't built up any strength or endurance yet.

Summary

The heart is a pump that sends blood around the body. When muscles are used, they need more oxygenated blood and therefore the heart must pump faster to supply it.

The Blood Vessels

Blood vessels are basically a network of thin pipes that take blood to every part of the body. They set off from the heart in quite large vessels called arteries, which then split down into arterioles and then further along their journey down into capillaries.

From here the blood penetrates into all the organs and tissues to deliver oxygen and take away carbon dioxide. The capillaries then continue to thread their way through the tissues until they merge into larger blood vessels called venules, which then in turn merge into the veins, which then finally return the blood to the heart.

The arteries and veins are the largest blood vessels but when it comes to importance with your training, the capillaries will have the greatest effect on your performance.

During endurance training something called capillarization occurs. This basically means your muscles will create more capillaries in the working muscles in an attempt to be able to cope with the challenges you are placing it under. This reaction is a direct response to the increasing demands you place on your body.

More capillaries means two things: firstly, the muscles will get a much faster and greater supply of oxygenated blood, and secondly, they also remove carbon dioxide and other waste products much quicker.

This is one of the reasons why your training needs to be gradual and progressive in order for your muscles to build up a need to create more capillaries.

Summary

Blood vessels are pipes of varying sizes that take blood around the body, away from the heart and then back to it again after delivering oxygen and collecting carbon dioxide and other waste products from the cells.

The Blood

When muscles contract they require a supply of proteins, vitamins, minerals, and oxygen which are all supplied in the blood through the arteries, arterioles, and capillaries. At this stage the blood is classified as oxygenated blood. After the oxygen has been delivered, the blood then takes away carbon dioxide and is now called deoxygenated blood. This isn't the only job the blood does; it also takes away waste products.

When muscles contract they create lactic acid and carbon dioxide, which need to be removed in order to maintain normal acid levels so that the muscles can continue to contract without fatiguing. The deoxygenated blood now absorbs these waste products and takes them away from the muscles through capillaries, venules, and veins, and back to the heart.

Summary

Blood is a transportation medium, a bit like a lorry: it delivers the things the muscles need, then it takes away any waste the muscles don't need.

The Respiratory System

This section is all about breathing and the role that the lungs play in providing oxygen to support the muscles.

Adapting and improving your circulatory (cardio) and respiratory (pulmonary) systems is something that should be a progressive process that happens over weeks, not just a few days.

Working in conjunction with the circulatory system, the respiratory system breathes in oxygen to the lungs and then breathes out carbon dioxide.

The first stage of oxygen transportation begins with breathing in or inhaling through the mouth or nose. The nose is the preferred option as it warms and filters the air on its way through. The air then passes through the larynx at the back the throat and then down through the trachea (windpipe).

The trachea then divides into bronchi and through progressively smaller tubes until it reaches the lungs. The lungs contain tiny air sacks called alveoli which allow gaseous exchange to happen whereby oxygen is diffused into the capillaries and exchanged with carbon dioxide, which is then returned to the lungs to be breathed out.

Alveoli have a surface area of around 70 square meters.

The process of breathing doesn't alter very much from rest to exercise, although there will be a need to use the mouth more than the nose when exercising. Although the nose provides cleaner and warmer air, it can't provide the increased volume of air needed for intensive exercise.

Summary

The respiratory system is mainly responsible for the intake of oxygen which is needed for muscles to work and expelling carbon dioxide, a waste product of muscular contraction.

The importance of the information we've just covered, understanding how the body works, cannot be understated as it describes the process of adaptation that these organs undergo and improve through training. For you to be able to run any distance, your circulatory and respiratory systems clearly need to change and become stronger and more efficient at their jobs. This will not only improve your performance and ability to run further but will also improve your long-term health and longevity.

The Muscles

The body contains over 600 muscles which are responsible for creating movement and stabilising the body. These muscles are made up of two different types of muscle fiber, known as fast twitch (type A) or slow twitch (type B).

Slow twitch muscle fibers contract slowly and are mainly used for activities that require slower, continuous movements, such as distance running. They are very good at utilising fat and carbohydrates for energy. As a runner it is these slow twitch muscle fibers that you will be training to make them more efficient and durable.

Fast twitch muscle fibers are called upon at times when you need your muscles to quickly contract such as power movements used in weight training and short sprints. They are called into action on these occasions because of their ability to contract and produce energy very rapidly.

Studies show that we have a predetermined amount of fast or slow twitch muscle fibers at birth; however, just because someone has a greater percentage of one type or the other does not mean that they can't excel in endurance training. Given regular stimulus for change, either type of muscle fiber has the ability to take on the characteristics of the other.

The Chemical Behind Movement

Your body is very much like a car in that it needs fuel to be able to move. The food you eat is to your body what petrol is to your car. When foods are eaten they are broken down into much smaller parts. I'll discuss this in more detail in the section on nutrition.

Depending on the type of exercise and level of intensity you work at will depend on the nature of the fuel source. Generally we use fats and carbohydrates that we eat to create the chemical we need to produce movement.

This chemical is called Adenosine Triphosphate (ATP). ATP cannot be stored in muscle as it is too unstable. It must be made on demand and is produced in a variety of ways depending on which type of activity is being performed. For slower paced exercises ATP is needed, but it isn't needed quickly, so it uses a mixture of carbohydrates and fats.

For faster bouts of exercise, such as sprinting, ATP is needed quickly in order to meet the increased oxygen demands from the muscles, so more enzymes are produced in order to produce more ATP. But this ATP is produced mainly from carbohydrates, due to the fact that fats aren't as easily accessible and they take longer to break down in order to be used in the production of energy.

The Endocrine System

The endocrine system is responsible for the secretion and regulation of a huge array of chemical messengers called hormones that keep the body in a permanent state of balance. Glands located all over the body are responsible for producing these hormones.

Your brain is ultimately in charge of maintaining the correct balance and production of hormones. A deficiency or over-production of one hormone can have a big impact on the balance of the entire hormonal system and as a result can cause changes in the way the body operates. This can lead to illness or negatively affect your ability to exercise effectively.

During exercise your hormone levels will change in response to the changing levels of oxygen, blood, and fluid levels. Perhaps the most relevant hormones to us as endurance runners are adrenalin and insulin.

Adrenalin

Adrenalin is responsible for a number of things, including elevating the heart rate and the conversion of carbohydrates into glucose which is needed to produce ATP (the chemical used to produce energy).

Adrenalin levels can rise and fall in response to any number of situations from anger to sadness to stress. Adrenaline is well known as the "fight or flight hormone" because it can quickly increase heart rate and energy production, giving you the ability to run faster or fight harder. It is usually only relied upon for explosive situations.

Insulin

Insulin is produced by the pancreas in order to maintain normal blood sugar levels, to either clear glucose from the blood if it gets too high (hyperglycaemia) or put glucose into the blood if glucose levels fall too low (hypoglycaemia). It is produced by the pancreas to remove sugars from the blood whenever carbohydrates are eaten. The insulin produced then moves that blood sugar to the muscles to be used as energy or stored in the liver. Some of this glucose may be left in the bloodstream to normalise blood sugar levels.

When the body produces excess insulin, this can cause too many carbohydrates to be stored, leaving little in the bloodstream. This in turn prompts the body to crave more carbohydrates to normalise blood sugar levels, and the same thing happens again. This cycle leads to an overconsumption of carbohydrate calories and a constant yo-yo effect on blood sugar levels.

During running, insulin levels can play a role in the effectiveness of your sessions. If you eat too many carbohydrates prior to a run it can lead to an increase in the production of insulin, which may result in a lower blood sugar content in the blood, leaving you feeling tired much sooner than normal. Eating a carbohydrate-rich meal 1 – 2 hours before training is ideal because you will boost your glycogen levels in the muscles without the sudden blood sugar spike and subsequent lowering of blood sugar levels you would experience if you ate immediately before exercise.

Your Body's Secret Saboteur

Unfortunately, one thing that you will not be able to control is your body's immune system. Because of the nature of your chosen sport (running), you may be at greater risk than most of suffering from infections and illness.

The reason for this is that after a long training session your immune system will be temporarily incapable of doing the job it should do properly (fighting off infection and germs). An increase in catecholamines and glucocorticoids is thought to be the reason behind this, as these chemicals suppress the immune system's ability to do its job.

This may be offset by consuming small amounts of carbohydrate drinks throughout your training.

Looking After Your Feet

Your feet are subjected to many thousands of steps each day, many more if you are running regularly. Occasionally your feet will rebel and complain. There are many foot and ankle injuries that can be attributed to running. One of the main problems that leads you to suffering these injuries can be poor foot position when landing.

Over-pronation of the foot, where the foot rolls inwards excessively which results in an unstable foot, increasing the force placed on supporting muscles.

Under-pronation (supination) of the foot is where the feet turn outwards excessively, again placing the muscles, tendons and ligaments at risk of overload and injury.

As well as the feet, the ankles also take a huge amount of stress. Studies have clearly shown that up to 60% of the impact of running is absorbed through the ankles.

When the position of the foot is compromised there is a much higher chance of stress fractures of the heel bone and metatarsals. But there are many other foot conditions that runners often complain about. Here are the most common.

Blisters

Blisters basically occur when layers of skin pull apart and fill up with fluid. This is caused by a buildup of heat due to friction or pressure. Here are some good tips to help you cope with blisters:

• Moisturize your feet before running to reduce the friction that leads to the formation of blisters.

- Applying a petroleum-based jelly to any problem areas before you start can also reduce friction and chafing of the skin.
- Wear nylon socks instead of cotton. Using a good pair of specialist running socks will also help.
- Choosing the right size of trainers when buying a new pair is very important. Allow for the swelling of the foot when running and select a size that is approximately a thumb's width longer than your actual size.

Bunions

A bunion is a structural deformity of the bones and the joint between the foot and big toe, thought by experts to be caused primarily by poorly fitting footwear. Specifically, a bunion is an enlargement of bone or tissue around the joint at the base of the big toe. The big toe may turn in towards the second toe, which causes inflammation in the tissues surrounding the joint which then become swollen and tender.

The symptoms of bunions can include:

- Irritated skin around the bunion.
- Pain when walking or running.
- Joint redness and pain.
- Possible shifting of the big toe inwards toward the other toes.

Bunions can be helped by a change in footwear or trainer selection or by using orthotics, which are basically splints or gel inserts that help to realign the toe positions. However, these treatments only address the symptoms and don't treat the cause. To correct this, surgery may be the only option.

Corns

Corns and calluses are a thickening of skin on the feet that can become painful. They are caused by excessive pressure or friction (rubbing) on the skin. The most common cause is poorly fitting shoes. Sometimes a rough seam or stitching in a shoe may rub enough to cause a corn. A podiatrist can par (cut away) corns and calluses and can advise on footwear, shoe insoles, padding, etc., to prevent recurrences.

Hard corns commonly occur on the top of the smaller toes or on the outer side of the little toe. These are the areas where poorly fitted shoes tend to rub the most.

Soft corns sometimes form in between the toes, most commonly between the fourth and fifth toes. These are softer because the sweat between the toes keeps them moist. Soft corns can sometimes become infected.

To relieve the pressure on the areas where the corns are forming, put padding between the toes or on top of them and consider buying a shoe with a larger toe box.

Calluses

A callus is larger, broader, and has a less well-defined edge than a corn. These tend to form on the underside of the foot (the sole). Commonly they form over the bony area just underneath the toes. This area bears much of the weight when we run. They may initially be painless but can become painful after a time. Treatment is similar to that of corns.

Ingrown toenails

Ingrown toenails are a common nail problem. This is usually a very painful condition in which the nail grows so that it cuts into one or both sides of the surrounding tissue.

Toenails can become ingrown if the nails are cut too short and rounded at the edges. As a result, the skin grows over the edge of the nail, creating a painful swollen area that may become infected. You can reduce and limit the effect of ingrowing toenails by:

• Cutting the nails straight across at the tip instead of cutting the nail too short, rounding off at the tip or peeled off at the edges.
• Choosing footwear that fits properly, as choosing shoes that are too narrow or too short can cause bunching of the toes, causing the nail to curl and dig into the skin.
• Avoid causing trauma to the nail or toe, which may be caused by stubbing the toenail, dropping things onto the toes, or damage caused through activities such as football. All these may result in injury to the surrounding skin, causing the flesh to become inflamed and the nail growing irregularly and pressing inwards.

Ingrown toenails can be a genetic problem or may be caused by disease.

In mild cases doctors recommend daily soaking of the affected digit in a mixture of warm water and Epsom salts and applying an antiseptic cream which may allow the nail to grow out so that it can be trimmed properly, allowing the flesh to heal.

Many ingrown toenails do not progress to infection stage, and occasionally heal themselves without intervention. However, a visit to a podiatrist is recommended if the swelling is severe, if there is pus or bleeding, or if the toenail remains ingrown for more than a few weeks.

Morton's Neuroma

This is a condition that affects one of the nerves that run between the metatarsal bones of the foot. The exact cause is not certain. Symptoms include pain, burning, numbness, and tingling between two of the toes of the foot. Tight shoes tend to worsen the pain since they put pressure on the inflamed nerve. The treatments for this condition are:

- **Calf-stretching exercises** which can help to relieve the pressure on your foot.
- **Steroid or local anesthetic injections** (or a combination of both) into the affected area of the foot. These may be needed if changes in footwear do not fully relieve the symptoms. However, footwear modification measures should still be continued.
- **Sclerosant injections** involve the injection of alcohol and local anesthetic into the affected nerve under the guidance of an ultrasound scan. Some studies have shown this to be as effective as surgery.
- **Surgery** - If non-surgical measures do not work, surgery is sometimes needed. Surgery normally involves a small incision being made on either the top, or the sole, of the foot between the affected toes. Usually, the surgeon will then either create more space around the affected nerve (known as nerve decompression) or will resect (cut out) the affected nerve. If the nerve is resected (cut out), there will be some permanent numbness of the skin between the affected toes, but this doesn't normally cause any major problems.

Athlete's foot

Athlete's foot is a fungal infection of the skin that causes scaling, flaking, and itching of the affected areas. It is usually passed on in moist areas where people walk barefoot, such as in showers, swimming pools, saunas, or steam rooms.

The infection thrives in warm, moist conditions and is often made worse by wearing tightly fitting running shoes. An itchy red rash between the toes is a common symptom.

Athlete's foot can be prevented by washing and drying your feet regularly and thoroughly, especially between the toes. Always replace previously-worn socks with freshly washed ones..

Treatment is usually an application of pharmaceutical creams and powders, which have a very good success rate, usually within a few weeks.

Plantar Fasciitis

Plantar Fasciitis is a common problem amongst runners. It affects the long band of connective tissue called the plantar fascia which supports the arch of the foot. The inflammation is often caused by heavy heel planting which compresses the area, or alternatively running too much on the toes, which can over-stretch the tissue.

The pain is usually felt on the underside of the heel and can usually be felt at its worst during the first steps of the day.

It is commonly associated with long periods of standing or sudden changes in weight bearing or activity. Jobs that require a lot of walking on hard surfaces, shoes with little or no arch support, a sudden increase in weight, and over activity are also common causes of the condition.

There are many ways to treat the problem, although really it is best to go to a physiotherapist who may recommend any of the following:

• Stretching of the Achilles tendon and plantar fascia.
• Staying off the feet as much as possible.
• Weight loss.
• The use of specially-designed arch supports and heel inserts.
• Strategically taping up the area to eliminate excessive stretching or compacting.

There are some things you can do yourself that can help to improve the condition. Here a few simple tips –

• Placing ice or a bag of frozen peas or sweet corn under the foot and rolling over the top provides a stretch and an ice treatment at the same time.
• Massaging the calf muscle just over the heel can relieve symptoms slightly.
• Scrunching up your toes into a tight ball and then releasing can make a difference. Hold the squeeze for a count of 5, then relax and repeat for 10 repetitions. Do this regularly throughout the day.

Stress fractures

A stress fracture is an overuse injury caused when muscles become tired and lose the ability to absorb the shock of your footfall. If you suffer from foot pain that gets worse as you run further, there is a good chance that you have a stress fracture. You will need to be referred for an MRI scan for a conclusive diagnosis as X-raying the foot doesn't tend to be able to clarify this.

These are sometimes referred to as hairline fractures. A stress fracture has the characteristics of a very small sliver or crack in the bone. They normally occur in weight-bearing bones, such as the tibia (bone of the lower leg) and metatarsals (bones of the foot).

It is a very common sporting injury, mostly associated with runners. The reason for this is down to muscle tiredness and fatigue. For every mile a runner runs, more than 110 tons of force must be absorbed by the legs. Bones aren't capable of withstanding that much impact on their own and rely on the surrounding muscles, which act as shock absorbers for the extra force.

Unfortunately, as the muscles become tired and stop absorbing most of the shock, the bones experience greater and greater amounts of stress. Eventually when the muscles (usually in the lower leg) become so fatigued that they stop absorbing any shock, all forces are then transferred to the bones. This is when stress fractures usually occur.

You can help to reduce the risk of suffering from stress fractures by strengthening the muscles of the lower legs such as the muscles down the front and back of the calves, the Tibialis Anterior and the Gastrocnemius and Soleus muscles. This will help them to absorb the strain of running for longer periods of time.

Stress fractures usually have only a few symptoms, such as pain or tenderness when weight bearing. Usually when running, a stress fracture in the leg or foot will cause severe pain at the beginning of the run, moderate pain in the middle of the run, and severe pain again afterwards.

If a stress fracture occurs in a weight-bearing bone, healing will be delayed or prevented if you continue to place stress and put weight on to that limb. Rest is the only option for complete healing of a stress fracture.

Recovery times vary depending upon the location of the fracture, its severity, and the ability of the body to be able to heal itself. Common healing times are between 4 to 8 weeks, although periods of rest of 12 to 16 weeks are not uncommon for more severe cases.

You should phase activity in very slowly after this period, provided the activity does not cause any pain. While the bone may feel healed and not hurt during daily activity, the full healing process may take many months after the injury feels better, and the chances of suffering refracture are quite high.

Since running places additional stress on the bone, it should only be resumed gradually, phasing in small amounts at a time, and increasing distances by no more than 10% each week.

Replacing your shoes regularly can help to avoid some of these injuries because of a loss of the support and cushioning in older shoes. Shoes that have little support can result in injuries such as plantar fasciitis, Achilles heel pain, knee pain and so on.

Good advice to adhere to is to replace your shoes every 350–400 miles.

Eating to Boost Your Performance

"If you're trying to achieve, there will be roadblocks. I've had them; everybody has had them. But obstacles don't have to stop you. If you run into a wall, don't turn around and give up. Figure out how to climb it, go through it, or work around it."

- Michael Jordan

Perhaps one of the most underestimated elements of running a 5k race and your training is the area of nutrition. Along with your training schedule, your diet needs a great deal of your time and attention if you want to perform your best.

Learn as much as you can about this topic and more importantly how it relates to your specifically. Try to find out as early in your training as possible which types of foods you can eat before running and which types cause you problems.

It is very important to base your dietary decisions purely on yourself and your own body. Many people take advice from fellow runners about the types of foods and liquids they consume before a race and then blindly follow that advice. The advice might not be wrong, but it is probably best suited to that particular person and not specifically for you.

With the help of this manual, you will be able to first identify the types of foods you should be consuming and then test their suitability to yourself.

There are three basic types of food that we consume in our diet, known as macronutrients – fats, proteins, and carbohydrates. During exercise your body will use all these nutrients in varying amounts depending on the length of time, speed, and type of activity you are involved in.

Here is a quick overview:

Fats

The fat we eat is broken down into fatty acids and then stored for energy all over the body. This energy supply is mainly used for exercise which requires a low amount of effort. As the intensity or difficulty of the exercise increases, there begins a shift in the ratio of fats and carbohydrates used.

Some fats are essential for us to consume in order to effectively absorb and utilize the vitamins ADEK we get from our foods.

Fats can be classed as saturated or unsaturated fats (poly and mono). It is the saturated fats that can be potentially harmful to us as their structure leads to a potential build up on the inside of the artery walls, leading to atherosclerosis or a narrowing of the arteries which increases blood pressure and may lead to heart disease.

Saturated fats are easy to spot because they are the types that turn solid at room temperature. They are mainly found in meat sources. Whilst it is virtually impossible to eliminate fat from your diet (and you do need some), it is a good idea to cut down on its consumption as much as possible. Here are some good tips to use to avoid eating too much saturated fat:

- Don't eat too much red meat; once or twice a week is more than enough.
- Drain away any excess fats that are produced from the cooking process.

- Grill or bake foods instead of frying.
- Remove visible fat from meat and poultry.
- Remove the skin from meat and poultry.
- Try to avoid foods made from a combination of meat sources such as burgers and sausages.
- Dairy products are also usually very high in saturated fats so try to avoid eating too much cheese, butter, cream, mayonnaise, etc.

Polyunsaturated fats have some very beneficial properties. For example, they provide us with the essential fatty acids such as omega 3 and omega 6. These fatty acids are derived mainly from fish and vegetable sources, and they help us to maintain the correct water balance in our body and regulate cholesterol levels and metabolic rate amongst other things.

Monounsaturated fats also provide an important role in our body. They can help to reduce the bad form of cholesterol levels we have in our blood. Olive oil is perhaps the best example of a good monounsaturated fat.

As a target, aim to eat no more than 20 - 25% of your total calories from fat, but bear in mind that 1g gram of fat contains 9kcals, as opposed to proteins and carbohydrates which contain just 4kcals per gram.

Protein

In relation to running, protein is mainly used for the rebuilding and repair of muscle damage caused through the action and byproducts of your training. In extreme circumstances, protein can also be used as a fuel source.

When proteins are digested, they are broken down into amino acids and then transported around the body to do the various jobs they need to do, whether that be to repair muscle tissue, renew skin cells, etc.

A diet that includes good-quality fish and meats will ensure that you are providing yourself with the optimum amount of protein in your diet. As a rule, try to include some form of quality protein in each meal which should ensure you are getting enough. Vegetarians will have to work much harder to ensure that they are getting enough of the right types of low-fat proteins in their diet.

Current recommendations are that you consume in the region of 1.5g of protein per kilogram of your own body weight per day. So, for a typical woman weighing 65kg she would need to eat around 97.5g of protein per day. (65kg x 1.5g = 97.5g)

Carbohydrates

Whilst not to underestimate the importance of the other nutrients, carbohydrates are possibly the most important food source to be aware of as a runner.

Carbohydrates should provide the body with at least 60% of its total daily calories. Their main use in the body is to provide us with energy.

When carbohydrates enter the body, they are converted to glucose before being used by the cells. Glucose is the only source of energy that the brain can use.

In terms of providing the body with the correct amount of carbohydrates there is no difference between simple and complex carbohydrates. The difference is that a potato (complex carbohydrates) will fill you up where as a few spoonfuls of sugar (simple carbohydrates) will leave you feeling empty and wanting more.

Some examples of simple carbohydrate sources include sweets, cakes, buns, biscuits.

Complex carbohydrates, especially in their natural form, can also provide the diet with protein, fiber, vitamins, and minerals, none of which can be found in sugar. Sugar provides empty calories. A continued overconsumption of sugar can lead to maturity-onset diabetes and may cause dental cavities.

It is quite difficult to over consume calories from complex carbohydrate sources because you will usually feel full first. However, if you do over consume calories over and above your daily requirements from whichever source, be it proteins, fats, **OR** carbohydrates, that excess will be stored on the body as fat.

Complex carbohydrates in the diet should be increased, whereas simple carbohydrates should be decreased. Eating a diet high in complex carbohydrates (high fiber) will make you feel fuller sooner and provide you with a constant and more regulated energy supply.

Complex carbohydrates provide dietary bulk or fiber, which leaves us feeling full and assists the digestive system. It is mainly found in the outer wall of foods and is therefore higher in those which are unrefined.

When carbohydrates are eaten, they are broken down into glucose which is then transported through the blood supply to be used as energy immediately or sent to the muscles for storage to be used as fuel in the future. Carbohydrates stored in our muscles are known as glycogen.

Glycogen has a very important role to play in the body. It is our primary fuel source due to the ease of its breakdown. Your body can store about 500g of glycogen, which would fuel approximately three quarters of the distance of a marathon. At this point your body must switch over to using proteins and fats for energy. Unfortunately, these substances take the body much longer to break down and create energy from, which means your performance will suffer and you will need to slow down or stop altogether. At this point if glycogen levels aren't topped up then there will be an insufficient supply of sugars to even keep the brain going, which is why you may have witnessed runners becoming dizzy and disoriented and possibly collapsing. This is known as hypoglycemia.

When running anything under 16 miles it is unlikely that you will deplete your glycogen stores and therefore suffer any of these side effects, but any distance above this requires that you absolutely must get your carbohydrate intake right, both before and during the race.

After your training you should always aim to eat a meal high in carbohydrates within an hour of finishing. The reason for this is that studies have shown that the body absorbs nutrients much quicker during this window to store as much fuel as possible for future usage.

Recommended Carbohydrates

Good choices	Fair Choices	Try To Avoid
Rice, Breads and Cereals		
Bagel	Muffin	Cakes
Couscous	Plain popcorn	Croissant
Pasta	Taco shells	Fried rice
Rice	Croutons	Pastries
Whole grains	Cereals	Sweet popcorn
English muffins	Pizza base	Crisps
Flour tortilla	Pancakes	Doughnuts
Vegetables		Fried tortilla
Vegetables		
Most vegetables served: -	Vegetables served with a	Coleslaw
Raw	reduced fat sauce	Chips
Steamed		Fried vegetables
Microwaved		Potato salad
All without butter, oil or		Mashed potatoes
salt added		
Vegetable juices		
Reduced fat vegetable		
soups		
Roasted vegetables in olive		
oil		
Fruits		
Fresh fruits	Olives	Avocados
Canned fruits in juices or		
water		
Fruit juice		

FIBER – This term describes foods that resist human digestive enzymes. Both types convey a feeling of fullness in the stomach because they absorb water. Some fibers delay the emptying of the stomach so you feel fuller for longer.

Insoluble fiber – does not dissolve in water in the stomach.
Soluble fiber – dissolves in water in the stomach.

Good choices of insoluble fiber

Apples, bananas, brown rice, cabbage, cauliflower, corn, bran, green beans, peas, legumes, nuts, cherries, citrus fruits, corn, rye, rice and wheat bran, root vegetables, pears, peaches, plums, seeds, tomatoes, strawberries, whole grain breads.

Good choices of soluble fiber

Apples, apricots, bananas, barley, broccoli, cabbage, carrots, peas, grapes, legumes, oat bran, pears, oatmeal, potatoes, prunes, seeds, sweet potatoes.

The Glycemic Index

The Glycemic Index, or GI as it is often referred to, is a measure of the effects of carbohydrates on blood glucose levels.

Carbohydrates that break down rapidly during digestion release glucose very quickly into the blood stream and are classified as being high GI foods.

Ideally, foods with a low GI are the best choices because these foods will release glucose more slowly and steadily. A high GI food causes a more rapid rise in blood glucose levels and is suitable for energy recovery after endurance exercise or for a person with diabetes experiencing hypoglycemia.

Here is an example of the GI values of some common foods:

Classification	GI Range	Examples
Low GI	55 or less	most fruit and vegetables (except potatoes, watermelon), grainy breads, pasta, legumes/pulses, milk, products extremely low in carbohydrates (fish, eggs, meat, nuts, oils), brown rice
Medium GI	56 - 69	Whole wheat products, basmati rice, sweet potato, table sugar, most white rices (eg, jasmine etc)
High GI	70 and above	corn flakes, baked potato, watermelon, croissant, white bread, puffed cereals (eg, Rice Krispies), straight glucose (GI = 100)

For anyone trying to lose weight, avoiding high GI foods is quite important as their aim is to maintain a constant blood sugar level so as to avoid feeling hungry and craving certain foods.

For anyone exercising regularly there is actually a benefit to eating high GI foods in order to replenish glycogen stores. This relates back to your body's need to quickly load up on fuel straight after exercise. High GI foods are absorbed much quicker into the bloodstream, thereby helping to quickly restock the glycogen lost through training.

Eating some fruit or a carbohydrate-based energy drink after training is an excellent way to replenish glycogen stores.

Hypoglycemia

Hypoglycemia is the medical term for a condition caused by lower-than-normal levels of blood glucose. The term hypoglycemia literally means "under sweet" blood.

Symptoms include:

● Shakiness, anxiety, nervousness, tremor

- Palpitations and tachycardia
- Sweating and a feeling of intense warmth
- Pallor, coldness, clamminess
- Dilated pupils (mydriasis)
- Feeling of numbness or pins and needles in the fingers

In addition to ensuring that you have consumed the correct amount of carbohydrates before your run, you can also:

- Carry a sports drink with you, or on race day make use of the sports drink stations.
- Take a carbohydrates gel with water every 45 minutes during your run.
- Snack on small sugary sweets; popular choices include jelly babies and jellybeans.

All the above suggestions should be tested before a race to ensure you suffer no reactions.

If you are a diabetic, you should consult a doctor before training and gain as much knowledge as you can about your condition and how running long distances will affect you.

While there is much debate regarding the proper mix of foods, try to aim for 65% of your total calories consumed coming from a variety of carbohydrate sources.

Emphasize healthy and nutritious foods in your diet while limiting your intake of fried and high fat foods.

The Importance of Fluids

During a typical 60-minute run you can lose anywhere between 1.5 – 3 liters of fluid through sweating alone. Once this water loss starts to happen, you will be at risk of dehydration. Continuing along this path without replenishing these fluids can lead to nausea, muscle cramps, dizziness, and confusion.

At an extreme of this point hyperthermia may set in. Hyperthermia is a condition which occurs when the body produces or absorbs more heat than it can get rid of.

One of the body's most effective methods of temperature regulation is perspiration, which draws heat from inside, allowing it to be dispersed outside the body.

Evaporation of sweat from the skin's surface also helps to cool the body down further, because this process draws yet more heat from the body. If someone becomes so dehydrated that they can no longer sweat, then this way of reducing body temperature is no longer available. At this point, core temperatures begin to rise quickly.

Replacing fluids is one of the most important factors you should consider when you are running. The amount you should drink depends on how much you lose.

A simple test is to weigh yourself before you start your run and then weigh yourself again at the end, in order to calculate the amount of fluid you typically lose. For example, let's say you weigh 75kg before you start. After an hour you reweigh yourself and this time you only weigh 74kg. This means that you have lost 1kg. 1kg of weight loss equates to 1 liter of fluid loss, so this gives you an indication as to the amount of fluid you need to drink during similar runs to maintain normal hydration levels.

You should aim to drink ½ - 1 liter of water up to an hour before running to ensure you are correctly hydrated.

Use the hydration chart below to monitor your urine color which will indicate your current fluid status. You should aim to stay within level 1 and 2. Colors 3 – 4 mean you are dehydrated and 5 – 6 severely so.

HYDRATION LEVELS					
1	2	3	4	5	6
IDEAL		DEHYRATED		SEVERELY DEHYDRATED	

Drinking During Your Run

Water is the ideal drink for everyday use and for runs lasting up to 90 minutes.

Sports drinks should be consumed (along with water) for runs over 90 minutes in duration, as they help to replenish glycogen stores. This is particularly important after 90 minutes of continuous exercise as this is the point when glycogen levels can become depleted.

Most sports drinks are specially designed to replace fluid and carbohydrates which they do very effectively, but they don't replace vitamins and minerals.

Choose drinks which contain both carbohydrates and sodium, but try them out first in smaller quantities before gulping down on a long run as they may cause stomach upsets and cramps. Take a few sips every 15-20 minutes during your run and remember that in very hot or humid weather you might need to drink more.

Unfortunately, there is only one thing you can do when you are severely dehydrated during a run and that is to stop running. If you don't stop, your body will eventually make its own decision to call it a day. You can avoid this state simply by staying well hydrated before you start and then regularly topping up your fluid levels as you run.

Drinking After Your Run

After running you should aim to replace any fluid loss as quickly as possible, drinking at least the amount you have lost in sweat.

The best choices for recovery fluids are fresh fruit juices such as orange, pineapple, and grape juice which supply carbohydrates, fluid, and electrolytes. If the juice is too acidic, try diluting it with water.

Water can replace fluids as well as any commercial sports drinks. When combined with a good diet, drinking water is more than capable of keeping your internal water levels balanced.

Don't rely on thirst to indicate signs of dehydration because it is very difficult to catch up on your fluid requirements once you sense that you are thirsty. For this reason, it is important to try and stay hydrated throughout the day.

But a word of warning: staying well hydrated during endurance exercise is very important, but drinking too much fluid can also be harmful and even potentially fatal. Hyponatremia, also referred to as "water intoxication," can occur when total fluid intake exceeds the amount of fluid lost during exercise, resulting in an imbalance between the body's water and sodium levels. This extreme condition can lead to nausea, fatigue, and vomiting and in the most severe instances, seizures, coma, and even death.

Optimum fluid levels are very important to runners for the following reasons:

- It helps us to get rid of heat through the skin by sweating.
- It helps the body to get rid of waste products and toxins in urine.
- It helps to transport glucose in the blood to our muscles so that we can exercise.

Without being correctly hydrated, the body cannot perform at its best and a dehydrated runner will end up performing well below their potential.

Here are some warning signs of dehydration:

- Feeling tired all the time
- Headaches
- Feeling generally weak

Recommended Sports Drinks

As mentioned already, a carbohydrate or sports drink is ideal for replacing glycogen stores during and after your runs, so here is a summary of the benefits of products on the market.

Sports drinks can be split into three major types:

Isotonic drinks

These drinks contain proportions of water and other nutrients similar to the human body, particles of carbohydrate and/or electrolytes which have the same concentration as the body's own fluids. This leads to an absorption rate similar to that of water. Isotonic drinks contain between 4g – 8g of sugar per 100ml. These are ideal for using before exercise.

Hypotonic drinks

Hypotonic drinks contain a greater proportion of water, and a lesser proportion of sugar, than the human body. They are less concentrated than the body's own fluids which allows them to be absorbed by the body much faster. This increased absorption rate helps to speed up the rehydration process. They typically contain less than 4g sugar per 100ml and because of their ability to quickly replenish glycogen stores, they are perfect for drinking during exercise.

Hypertonic drinks

The last category of sports drinks is classified as hypertonic. These drinks contain a lesser proportion of water, and a greater proportion of sugar, than the fluids in the body. They are more concentrated than the body's fluids and are absorbed at a slower rate. They usually contain more than 8g sugar per 100ml and are best used as a recovery drink after exercise or when you don't require quick rehydration.

Avoid the following drinks

- Alcohol
- Caffeine-based drinks
- Carbonated or fizzy drinks

Don't wait until you feel thirsty before you drink, as at this point you may already be dehydrated. Here are a few suggestions to get your fluid intake correct:

- Drink regularly throughout the day; up to 2 liters is recommended.
- Sip small amounts of water regularly over the course of your runs if less than 60 minutes and a carbohydrate-based sports drink for any that last longer than this.
- Water is the best choice of fluid, as this doesn't contain added extras such as sugar, fats, alcohol, or caffeine.

Supplements For Runners

"We are different, in essence, from other men. If you want to win something, run 100 meters. If you want to experience something, run a marathon."

- Emil Zatopek

For many runners and keen sportspeople, it is tempting to believe that there supplements out there that can radically improve your ability to run faster and further. Any supplements that claim this must be researched and considered very carefully as some supplement manufacturers use questionable testing techniques and misleading implied benefits on the packaging of their products.

Claims are often very flimsy with only anecdotal evidence provided, showing only the select few positive findings and making no mention of all the negative results also found.

The following are the supplements I recommend as they all have a proven track record and may be able to provide some benefits to your training.

Carbohydrate Supplements

Carbohydrate supplements based on glucose polymers are very useful for postponing fatigue and improving endurance during longer bouts of exercise, typically 60 -90 minutes and over. They are often sold in the form of powders, gels, tablets, and pre-mixed drinks and bars. Always take these with water to avoid stomach cramps and to improve absorption into the blood stream, unless you are using the premixed drink version.

These supplements provide carbohydrates that can be rapidly absorbed in the blood stream, thus replenishing glycogen stores. This is very useful, if not vital, for any runs that last longer than 60-90 minutes.

If you are on a calorie-controlled diet, be wary as you will be adding many more calories to your daily intake if you do use these supplements regularly.

To be perfectly honest, you wouldn't need to use these supplements any times other than when you are training or immediately afterwards. They do contain quite a lot of sugars and are normally high in calories.

Vitamin Supplementation

Regular and intense exercise increases the body's need for many vitamins and minerals. This need can largely can be met by consuming a well-balanced diet rich in fresh fruits, vegetables, and lean cuts of meats, poultry, and fish. However, insuring against any possible deficiencies by taking a multivitamin is a good idea.

There is also a single vitamin that a regular runner may benefit from: vitamin C.

Vitamin C

This vitamin is responsible for maintaining a healthy immune system, helps to improve the absorption of iron, wards off infection, and is an antioxidant (a vitamin that helps to seek out and neutralize the negative effects of the byproducts of movement and exercise, amongst other things).

As mentioned earlier, after longer runs your body's immune system is severely compromised, leaving you susceptible to any bugs going around, including colds and viruses. Supplementing with 1000mg of vitamin C per day is the optimal dosage, although the recommended daily allowance is much lower than this total.

Caffeine

If you decide to use this supplement, it should be used sparingly. I recommend testing it in small amounts during your training to see if you notice any benefits. Certainly avoid taking in large doses and be wary of dehydration.

Caffeine is a stimulant that can be found in teas, coffee, and some soft drinks. High doses can increase the amount of fat you burn for energy instead of glycogen during aerobic exercise, meaning your glycogen stores may last for longer. The benefits of caffeine become less noticeable when used on a regular basis. For example, anyone who drinks many cups of coffee or tea a day probably won't notice much of a difference at all.

The downside is that caffeine is a diuretic which means drinking too high a quantity could lead to dehydration which will compromise your training, so it is very important to stay well-hydrated. It can also cause headaches, dizziness, and nausea.

Using the Mind to Run Faster, Further, and Easier

"I always loved running...it was something you could do by yourself, and under your own power. You could go in any direction, fast or slow as you wanted, fighting the wind if you felt like it, seeking out new sights just on the strength of your feet and the courage of your lungs."

- Jesse Owens

Anyone that attempts to become proficient at any sport requires a certain strength of character and mental durability. Your body will certainly not want to go through the constant stress of running. Your mind will also rebel, seeking to provide logic and justification for the challenge you are placing yourself under.

Even if you're physically ready on race day, in good health and well-prepared, standing at the starting line mentally unprepared can have a negative effect on your performance.

But fear not, there are a number of mental strategies that you can use which will help you to prepare for these times and provide you with the mental strength to keep going when times are tough. Here are some of the most effective techniques:

Visualization

Visualization is the process of creating pictures and images in your mind which relate to the desired outcome. Examples of this would be:

Picturing yourself crossing the finishing line. Visualizing the cheering crowd and the other runners who have just completed their run. Picturing the clock displaying your desired finish time.

Self Talk

This strategy involves creating a positive voice that you can hear in your head providing motivation, support, and encouragement, very much like you would expect to hear from a personal trainer. When using self talk, try to talk to yourself in a positive and encouraging way.

Examples of effective and constructive self-talk would be:

"I am unique and special for training as hard as I am doing."
"I can keep on going just a bit longer."
"In another ten minutes I will have finished this run and I will feel amazing when I have had a shower and something to eat."
"I am not going to give up now because if I do, I will be so disappointed in myself."

Imagery

With regards to your training, imagery can be used to run through specific situations in your mind such as imagining your fastest run before you attempt it or imagining how your friends will react when you tell them that you have completed your first 5k race. Examples of imagery are:

- Imagine that you are running on air and your feet feel as though they are wrapped in cotton wool.
- Imagine that you are at the front of the race with all the other runners fading further and further into the distance behind you.
- Imagine that you are running effortlessly and feeling relaxed.

Another strategy is to take some time before your training run or race to consider all the possible problems that you might have. If you run a certain route and there are parts of it that are particularly challenging then rehearse how you will cope with and run through these difficult parts beforehand.

If you mentally rehearse the route and picture yourself running strongly and confidently around the course and finishing happily, it's much more likely to happen that way on the day.

The brain finds it difficult to distinguish between real and imagined memories, so if you haven't experienced something before, simulate it in your mind instead. This way, if it happens on the day, it won't feel new to you.

For example, let's say your goal is to complete a 5k race. The chances are that you have watched TV coverage of the event in the past. Draw on those images stored in your mind to pre-play the occasion so it doesn't feel so alien and unnatural on the day.

To be able to take on the challenge of completing a 5k race, you need to have certain characteristics such as motivation, self-discipline, and determination.

A positive mental attitude is also very important, and this will help you to complete the race, especially the latter stages which are usually the hardest part.

If you are worried about getting stressed out on race days or before your longer runs, you can try this simple relaxation technique:

Find somewhere quiet and relaxing and make yourself comfortable. Now think of a relaxing environment in your mind. It might be a place that you associate with special memories, or it might be a warm sandy beach where the sun is shining. Try to imagine the bright sun and clear blue sky, the feel of the warm sand underneath your feet, the sound of the sea lapping on the shore...

Studies have shown that using this technique can actually lower the heart rate quickly, but the secret is to master it and practice, practice, practice.

Reframing

Another technique is reframing. With reframing, the trick is to turn any negative thoughts into positive ones instead. An example of this would be when you are tired to such an extent that you feel like you need to stop. Instead of giving in and stopping, focus on all the times you've run that far before, as well as all the other training you've done in preparation.

When you catch negative thoughts entering your mind, quickly change them to positive affirmations such as:

Negative thought – "I really need to stop. I feel so tired."

Positive thought – "I am going to make myself really proud of what I can achieve by keeping going even when I feel a little bit tired. I can do this."

Thought Reversal

This type of technique is also known as "thought stopping". The secret is as soon as you start hearing negative thoughts, quickly replace them with a word or phrase like "stop," "no," "move on," or "change." Any word or short phrase will do as long as it triggers a change in your thought process.

Disassociation

Disassociation is the process of distracting yourself by taking your mind away from what your body is going through.

This can be used if you feel bored during your runs or if you are experiencing discomfort, tiredness, etc.

Listening to music on headphones is a very good way to take your mind off your running. It doesn't have to be just music you listen to, it could be comedy, positive thinking, or self-improvement techniques, anything that can keep your mind occupied.

If you don't like the idea of not being able to hear things around you, you could try any number of mind games such as:

Counting the number of cars you pass, or a basic alphabet game, where you pick a category (for example, countries, then run through the alphabet from A to Z, coming up with an answer for each letter. (Afghanistan, Belgium, Croatia, Denmark, you get the idea!)

On your longer runs try to break up the route into smaller chunks from one landmark or place to another, instead of thinking of completing the entire route in one go. When you reach the first landmark, then mentally think of running to the next, and so forth.

The prospect of an upcoming race can be quite worrying and stressful, so it's important to make sure you can relax properly on your rest days.

This exercise derived from neuro-linguistic programming is a great idea to help you here:

Sit or lie down comfortably in a quiet and relaxing place and try to remember a time when you felt really happy and content. Fully return to it now and try to see what you saw, hear what you heard, and smell what you smelled. Remember how good it felt.

Keep repeating these thoughts in your mind and make them bigger, brighter, and more intense. Try to smile as you increase the depth of these feelings, a big smile that extends right across your face from ear to ear, still thinking about these happy thoughts in your mind.

Next, gently squeeze your thumb and forefinger together at the same time as thinking intensely about this positive thought.

Continue to practice this technique regularly so that simply the action of squeezing your finger and thumb together will bring back those good feelings.

Conclusion For Section 1

"You see, in life, lots of people know what to do, but few people actually do what they know. Knowing is not enough! You must take action."

- Anthony Robbins

Well, there it is, all the basic knowledge you need to understand exactly what you are trying to encourage your body and mind to do. I have tried to make it as straightforward as I can, but there are certain sections where really the only way to describe things is in their scientific way.

Read this manual a couple of times until it sinks in properly and you actually 'get' it.

Simple things, such as how your muscles, heart, and lungs respond to exercise, are critically important for you to know if your aim is build up your mileage to be able to run 3.1 miles in one go.

You're now done with the theory and it's time to move on to Section 2 - The Practice. Let's get started on the physical journey towards your goal of running a 5k race.

Section 2 - The Practice

"Create a definite plan for carrying out your desire and begin at once, whether you're ready or not, to put this plan into action."

- Napoleon Hill

In the second part of this manual, you will discover the techniques and tips you need to take your goal of running a 5k race from contemplation stage to the practical, physical part of building up your fitness levels and training intensity to successfully run a 5k.

I would just like to recap where you should be at this point:

● You've decided you want to run a 5k.
● You have done some looking around and decided to buy this program; you've read through the theory manual and now understand the role your heart, lungs, and body play in enabling you to increase your running distances.
● You've sat down for an hour or so and written out some SMART goals that give you motivation towards achieving them.
● You've read about nutrition and understand the importance of carbohydrates in fuelling your body and allowing you to run further and recover faster.
● You've read all about injuries and learnt some strategies of how to avoid the most common problems when you start to increase how much training you do.
● Finally, you've looked at the type of tools you might need to help monitor and record your progress and the training gear you might need to buy.

• At this stage you may have even been to a specialist running shop in order to analyse your running gait so you are equipped with the right type of running shoes for your needs.

There's just one more thing you need to do...and that is to actually start training.

This manual provides you with all the information you need to get started including a number of advanced training techniques which you can use to boost your fitness levels far more quickly than just running at a fixed pace. There is also a section on stretching. Finally, I will walk you through your preparation and training right up to race day and beyond.

Have a good read through this manual, make notes where you need to, and then the big step: TAKE ACTION! Regular, consistent, and determined action towards your goal...

...Running your first 5k race.

How Difficult Should It Feel?

Training to run a 5k can be a very rewarding and enjoyable process. It shouldn't be a chore that you hate doing or a punishment that you need to suffer in order to help you to lose weight or get fit.

But to get this satisfaction you need to set some structure to your training. You can achieve this by following a progressive training program that allows you to improve constantly without risking overuse injuries or illness.

By ticking off goals and mini targets along the way to completing your first 5k, you will start to feel a sense of accomplishment and satisfaction from your efforts. The opposite is also true. Without doing this you will quickly become demotivated and bored with your training.

The right intensity is vitally important. If you don't work hard enough you will never make any real progress, whereas if you work too hard you run the serious risk of overtraining, injury, and extreme fatigue.

Neither of these outcomes are ideal, but both can be avoided.

During your training you will need to perform some sessions at different intensities to make steady and constant progress.

Running longer distances at a comfortable pace will allow you to improve your endurance, and running shorter distances at higher levels of intensity will build up leg strength and improve your body's ability to remove lactic acid from the muscles much faster, allowing you to work harder for longer. This is ideal if your chosen race includes any hills or gradients.

Aerobic Exercise

The American College of Sports Medicine (ACSM) defines aerobic exercise as "any activity that uses large muscle groups, can be maintained continuously, and is rhythmic in nature." It is a type of exercise that causes the heart and lungs to work harder than in everyday life.

Aerobic exercise basically means exercising in the aerobic training zone (a level at which your heart beats faster than in normal life and for a prolonged period of time). At this level of difficulty you should still be able to hold a conversation with someone quite easily. Once your speed or distance begins to increase so that you are no longer able to talk, you are moving past the aerobic threshold and towards anaerobic training (a level of training whereby the demand for oxygen from the muscles is far greater than that being supplied to them).

Aerobic (or endurance) training improves the endurance of your heart and lungs by increasing both the amount of blood that the heart can pump and your muscles' ability to extract oxygen from that blood. Any running program should be designed to improve your cardiovascular endurance, overload your heart and lungs, and improve your muscles' ability to utilize oxygen efficiently.

As with all training programs, specificity is crucial. If you are a runner and want to improve your ability to run, then you need to do plenty of running. Likewise, if you are a cyclist who wants to become more proficient at cycling up hills, then that's where you need to spend most of your training time.

Target Heart Rate Zones

To reap the most cardiovascular benefits from your workout, it is necessary to exercise within a recommended intensity range.

To arrive at a given intensity range for your level of effort, it is important to have a starting point. A standard way to measure this is to estimate your maximum heart rate (Max HR) and use this as a starting point.

The formula used to arrive at this figure is simply to subtract your age from 220.

For example, if you are 30 years old, your predicted maximum heart rate per minute is 190 (this is calculated as follows: 220 - 30 = 190) Your target heart rate is simply a certain percentage of this maximum heart rate.

Target Heart Rates will vary for each individual depending on age, current level of conditioning, and personal fitness goals but generally speaking for 5k steady state training, I'd like your exercising heart rate to range from between 50% to 70% of your maximum heart rate.

You can use the following chart to determine your predicted Target Heart Rate.

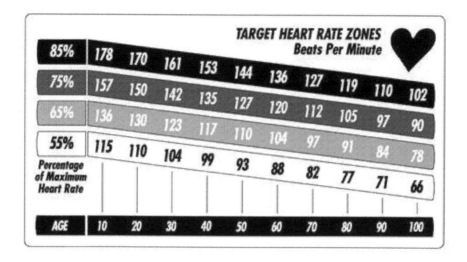

AGE	10	20	30	40	50	60	70	80	90	100
85%	178	170	161	153	144	136	127	119	110	102
75%	157	150	142	135	127	120	112	105	97	90
65%	136	130	123	117	110	104	97	91	84	78
55%	115	110	104	99	93	88	82	77	71	66

TARGET HEART RATE ZONES — Beats Per Minute

Percentage of Maximum Heart Rate

The heart rate zones as shown above are given the following meanings:

55% (50 – 60%) - Aerobic Beginners Zone
65% (60 – 70%) - Fat Burning Zone
75% (70 – 80%) - Aerobic Fitness Zone
85% (80 – 90%) - Peak Performance Zone

Ideally you want to be working generally within these parameters, so using our example above, your aerobic heart rate training zone range is 95 to 171, which is 50% - 90% of 190 (Max Heart Rate).

Obviously to accurately measure your heart rate during exercise you will need to purchase a heart rate monitor. There is no way of using this system otherwise.

If this sounds a little too technical for you then there is a much easier way of monitoring the intensity of your training called the rate of perceived exertion or RPE scale.

Rate of Perceived Exertion (RPE)

The Rate of Perceived Exertion (RPE) is one of the easiest ways to monitor exercise intensity. By using the RPE scale, you can continually assess your level of intensity during your workouts and ensure you are working at a level of effort or intensity that is comfortable and appropriate for you.

You can use the RPE scale on its own or with a heart rate monitor. An increase in exercise intensity will always lead to an increase and elevation in your heart rate and consequently your rate of perceived exertion (how difficult you find it).

There are a number of ways of interpreting the RPE scale, but I like to use the scale below as I feel this is more easily understood than other versions which use numbers up to 20 to gauge intensity.

RPE SCALE

1	Don't feel anything
2	Not at all challenging
3	Starting to feel something
4	Notice some effort
5	Feeling moderately challenging
6	Getting harder
7	Feeling quite hard
8	Feels very hard
9	Becoming very, very hard
10	That's it - you absolutely have to give up NOW!

Using the RPE scale as above, the recommended range during the majority of your training runs is between 5 (moderate) and 7 (feeling quite hard). Some training techniques will obviously require you to work harder than this and these are outlined in the training techniques section.

Building Stamina, Strength, and Fitness

The key to successfully training for a 5k is to safely and effectively build up your endurance and your body's ability to be able to cope with the constant impact that running can place upon it.

You can achieve both of these outcomes by making small and gradual increases to both the distances you run and the speed you run at.

As a general rule, you should increase your weekly mileage by no more than 10%. So for example, if you ran 10 miles in week 1, you shouldn't increase the mileage in week 2 by any more than an extra mile. (10% of 10 miles = 1 mile. Don't worry, I am not expecting you to run 10 miles in week 1, it's just for illustration purposes!)

As a first time 5k runner my advice is just try to simply complete the race without stopping. You don't need to worry about your speed or finishing in a certain time. If this is something you'd like to focus on, however, I have included a section for running the fastest time you can.

Lactate Threshold Training (Also referred to as anaerobic threshold training)

The lactate threshold is the point at which your body can no longer remove the buildup of lactic acid (an acid waste product created by your muscles contracting) in your muscles at the rate your muscular contractions are creating it, meaning you have to stop completely or at least reduce the intensity substantially.

When you exercise below the lactate threshold, any lactate created by the muscles is simply removed by the body without it building up.

The lactate or anaerobic threshold is considered to be somewhere between 90% and 95% of your maximum heart rate.

When you train at a higher level than your lactate threshold for any amount of time, such as sprinting or running up hills, lactic acid accumulates in the muscles to such an extent that you are forced to stop. By pushing yourself to this intensity regularly you can increase the body's ability to be able to remove lactic acid much faster and therefore do more and run further in future sessions.

The fitter you are and the more you push yourself out of your comfort zone, the higher your lactate threshold will be. By adding sessions into your program regularly that challenge you in this way, you will be improving your ability to do more.

Top endurance athletes regularly train at or above their lactic acid threshold in order to improve their capacity for working at higher intensities without lactate buildup during competition.

Interval training is a good way to improve your anaerobic threshold because it takes advantage of the fact that the body is pushed temporarily over the lactate threshold, and then able to recover whilst working below the lactate threshold at the same time as staying physically active as opposed to having to stop.

Apart from the obvious benefits of adding variety to your program, speed work, lactate threshold training and interval work can help you to run further and overcome gradient and speed challenges much easier.

Improving Your Running Technique

We have already discussed how to test your running gait and select trainers to suit that particular style in the theory manual, but if you are going to be running regularly, it is important that your technique is just right.

Here are a few tips to help you support and protect your body effectively when running:

- Aim to run tall with your head held high.
- Keep your shoulders back and down, with your chest out and stomach muscles pulled in tight and held there.
- You should run with a mid-foot to toe action: your mid-foot or heel contacts the ground first and then you roll forwards onto your toes before pushing off again.
- Your feet should be pointing slightly out to the sides.
- Use your arms to power you along, but try to relax your shoulders and keep them level.

Going Up a Gear - Advanced Training Techniques

I have included a number of advanced running training techniques for you to use, depending on which program you decide to follow. Using these techniques is beneficial to you for these reasons:

• Keeps your training fresh and enjoyable.
• Ensures that your body is given regular stimulation for change.
• Above all, dramatically boosts fitness levels far more quickly than simply running at the same pace and in similar circumstances each session.

These training techniques can feel quite hard, but it's absolutely vital to push yourself a little further than you can comfortably go in order to improve your ability to do more in the future. In fact, pushing yourself beyond your comfort zone is the only way you will ever improve.

Not doing this means you will stagnate and never increase your mileage or endurance.
Building up your endurance by gradually increasing the distances you run is just one way of improving your fitness. To do this effectively and as quickly as possible you can use a selection of the following advanced running techniques. They can also be used to add variety and to break through plateaus.

These techniques should be used in moderation and as a replacement for any of your weekly runs, not in addition to. Here they are:

Hill Reps

If you are lucky enough (or unlucky enough?) to live near or on some hills, then you can start to use these in your training. Hill training offers a great way to add intensity and build up power and strength in the legs. Also, many 5k races are set over undulating terrain so training using hills is a good way to prepare for your race.

Adding hill reps to your running program adds a much-needed dimension to a longer run, allowing muscle groups to function at anaerobic levels for a short period of time. In addition, hills and off-road running strengthen the muscles and connective tissues surrounding the ankles, an area that is subjected to a large amount of stress when running because the ankles provide balance and stability to the whole body.

Obviously if you live in an area where there aren't any hills you can't do this outside, so use a treadmill either at home or at your local gym. If you can't access any of these then just use pyramid training instead. Using a treadmill for some of your running is actually quite a good idea because of the reduced impact on your joints due to the cushioned effect of the treadmill running belt and bed.

Running hills can help in the following ways:

- Develops control and stabilization (downhill running)
- Promotes strength and endurance in the legs (uphill running)
- Helps to develop maximum speed and power
- Improves the body's ability to handle lactic acid

In order to do hill reps, select a hill or a section of a hill that will take you approximately 1 – 2 minutes to run up, the steeper the better. You'll be running up this at tempo pace, so don't go too far to begin with.

Run uphill at tempo pace and then simply walk back down or jog very gently, probably best to walk though to protect your joints. Before you start your hill reps you will need to warm up properly. Brisk walking up the hill and then stretching should be fine. Remember to also cool down at the end, again followed by stretches. The rest of the time should be work/rest time. Rest between hill reps should be long enough to reach a comfortable 5/6 on the RPE scale and allow your breathing rate to lower considerably. Whether this takes 5 minutes or just 30 seconds, wait until you have recovered.

Make a note on your training log of the times you run each rep, how long you rest for, and how many reps you manage to do in the allotted workout time.

Sprints

Sprints are a very demanding but absolutely great way to improve your distance running speeds. Sprinting increases your lactate (anaerobic) threshold and promotes better blood flow to the muscles allowing more nutrients to be delivered quickly and transporting away more waste, making your body much more effective at running for longer distances.

Sprinting uses energy systems that fatigue very quickly and leads to fast lactic acid build up in your muscles, causing you to need to slow down and stop.

The benefits of sprinting are:

● Increased running speed - allows for faster distance runs

- Raises the body's lactate threshold allowing you to run faster before lactic acid levels cause you to have to stop.
- Improves blood flow to the muscles meaning more oxygen reaches the muscles allowing them to function better.
- Improved aerobic capacity, allows the body to utilize oxygen more efficiently for prolonged periods of time.

It's absolutely vital to spend at least 10 minutes thoroughly warming up and stretching off both before and after a sprinting session.

The distance you choose is up to you, but bear in mind that you won't be able to run all-out for much longer than 10 - 15 seconds. Choose a distance between 50 and 100 metres and vary this according to your level of fitness.

After your warmup you should perform a couple of sprints at ¾ pace before going on to your all-out sprints. Allow a couple of minutes of active rest and stretching in between each sprint.

Regarding how many sprints to do, simply complete as many sprints as you can in the given workout time. For example, if the session length is 35 minutes, this will allow for a 10-minute warm up and a 10-minute cool down at the end, so the actual workout time should be around 15 minutes. Basically, you should complete as many sprints as you can during that time.

Allow yourself enough recovery time in between sprints.

Because of the dynamic nature of this type of training, it really isn't suitable for anyone from the age of 50 upwards. If you are over 50, instead of all-out sprinting you will get a very similar training effect by running your sprints at ¾ pace.

Make a note of how many sprints you manage to do during the session in your workout log. If you record the time for each one, this will give you something to aim to beat on subsequent sprint workouts.

Be wary as this type of intense training really does take it out of your legs. You will almost certainly feel some muscle soreness for a few days afterwards. Make sure you stretch thoroughly and allow enough recovery time before you train again.

Interval Training

Using interval training in your workouts is a great way to increase your anaerobic threshold, because it allows you to take periods of relative rest after periods of higher intensity exercise. This helps your body to clear lactic acid away from the working muscles, leaving your legs ready to continue further. With intervals there are many ways you can organise the session and it really is up to you. The main point to remember is that there should be a definite structure to the session, which should be decided beforehand.

The typical interval training approach is to begin with a rest/work ratio of 4:1, then the following week as your fitness improves 3:1, then 2:1 and so on. Use this basis if you like, or change to suit your preferences.

Also, you are not limited to intervals of hard and easy running. You may for example decide that you would like to use the following system:

Walk 1 minute, jog 1 minute, and then run ¾ pace for 30 seconds. It really is up to you. Make sure you record the details of your workout in your training log and subsequent sessions are increased by either the time, as I have shown, or the level of intensity you use.

One example might be that you walk slowly to one lamp post, then quickly to the next, then slowly again, and so on. Both the distance and speed can be changed to add variety to your workouts. Shorter, more intense intervals, such as sprinting, call for a much faster production of energy, which is why higher intensities can only be sustained for a short amount of time.

Using interval training in your program means that you can often reduce the volume of training and still see greater improvements in your fitness levels and running performance.

A longer working interval requires a greater involvement of aerobic energy production. This is because longer intervals need to be slightly lower in intensity than shorter ones for you to be able to carry on.

The recovery interval could consist of brisk walking or light jogging to bring down your heart rate, ideally to an RPE of approximately 6/10 by the end of the recovery bout. As you get fitter, your heart rate will drop much faster, allowing you to recover more efficiently.

Depending on your fitness level you will want to choose a work to recovery ratio that is suitable for you. For instance, as you get fitter aerobically, you won't need as much recovery time as you would when you first started. Beginners should use a rest/work recovery ratio of 4:1. This means that you might walk for 4 minutes and then run for 1 minute. As you improve your ability to run longer distances, your work intervals should generally last longer than 2 minutes to maximize the involvement of your aerobic energy system.

The benefits of interval training are:

- A very efficient and effective method of burning fat and boosting metabolic rate.
- Improves maximum oxygen uptake and increases fitness levels.
- Improves the anaerobic threshold.
- Interval training, whilst being more challenging, is much less monotonous compared to steady state training.

Fartlek Training

Fartlek training is basically playing with speeds, an advanced training technique which relies on your own judgement and level of fatigue. It's a great way to move your training forwards, without the structure needed for interval training.

The idea behind Fartlek training is to run throughout the session, but intersperse your normal pace with periods of faster running, as and when you feel sufficiently capable of doing so.

Fartlek is a Swedish word meaning "speed play." The use of Fartlek came about to provide a less structured approach than that of interval training. The benefits of this type of training are that it allows you to be able to increase or lower the intensity of your training depending on how you are feeling. You can control the session according to your levels of discomfort instead of having to work to a given point, be that a set time or a distance as you must do when using interval training.

Fartlek training is generally used to improve aerobic fitness and your ability to cope with higher levels of lactic acid build up in the muscles. It combines fast and slow running within a continuous run. Stages of faster running are followed by easy recovery running. The length of speed bursts and recovery should be unstructured so that you can get a real feeling of playing with speed.

Fartlek has grown into a popular method of training used by runners to provide an enjoyable and constructive alternative to simply pounding the streets with no purpose or plan.

Since the aim of Fartlek training is to develop speed in the context of long-distance running, the general pace should be relatively easy, although the overall effect of this type of training is far from easy.

Only the speed bursts should be done with any intensity. These short bursts of speed should only be around 30 seconds to 1 minute to begin with, increasing as you become fitter. However, you won't be timing this; instead you'll be gauging how it feels and slowing down when you feel you need to. Remember, you must leave yourself enough time between each higher-paced burst so that you can fully recover in between.

Fartlek training sessions should be quite short in nature as they are much more intense than continuous training. Sessions should typically last between 20 – 45 minutes.

Cross Training

Cross training is simply the use of a number of different types of exercise in an attempt to improve your aerobic ability. Basically, this is anything that challenges your heart a little to improve fitness levels and the strength and endurance of the heart and lungs.

The benefits of cross training are that using a wide range of activities to improve fitness levels keeps workouts fresh and enjoyable. This variety also removes much of the stress that occurs to muscles and joints when continually performing the same activities.

Single sports programs can often lead to muscle imbalances and repetitive motion injuries. With cross training there is much less likelihood that these injuries will occur due to the variety and range of different muscle groups involved.

Cross training can provide a flexible method of training which takes into account how you feel, your moods, and energy levels.

Aim to get out of your comfort zone and push yourself towards new highs. Don't be content to simply go through the motions with your cross training; it's okay to do that sometimes, but to get the most benefit, you'll need to progress in some way with each workout.

For your choices of cross training, you could row, swim, cycle, do an aerobics class, use an elliptical trainer, etc. If you choose to do this at a gym, you can use any number of pieces of equipment in one session or just stay on one, it's up to you. What I want here is for you to perform a different type of activity which still improves the strength and endurance of your cardiovascular system (heart, lungs, and circulation), without placing the same stresses on the joints and muscles that repetitive exercise can do.

Building up the session length will increase your endurance, helping you to increase your distances.

You will notice that all the programs I've designed contain cross training at some point or another.

Pyramid Training

Pyramid training is a way of gradually increasing your exercise intensity. Begin at a gentle pace and gradually increase the speed to a peak in the middle. Then gradually slow the pace back down to the end of the session. The secret here is to work very hard in the middle for a short period of time only, building up from the beginning and tapering down towards the end.

You will need to use a heart rate monitor or the RPE scale to do this type of training.

Initially you will need to work out your heart rates for each increase. Work out 50-60%, 60 -70%, 70 – 80% and 80 – 90% of your maximum heart rate.

You can use this formula: 220 – Your age = maximum heart rate.

As an example, a man who is 50 years old has a maximum heart rate of 170 (220 – 50). So to work out 50 % of his maximum heart rate you can simply divide 170 ÷ 10 and then times this by 5. 17 x 5 = 85.

If our 50-year-old man wants to work at 50% of his maximum heart rate, he would need to keep his heart rate at or around 85 beats per minute (BPM).

To start pyramid training, you should warm up gently for about 5 minutes and then start your training using 2 – 5 minutes in each heart rate or RPE zone building up to a peak at RPE 9/10 or 80 – 90% of your maximum heart rate in the middle of your session and then working back down again, finishing with a cool down and stretch of all the major muscles worked. A typical 24-minute pyramid workout for our example 50-year-old male would look something like this: -

220 – 50 = 170 maximum heart rate

% Max Heart Rate	Your Heart Rates(Bpm)/RPE Scale (example 50 year old)	Time
5 minute warm up		
50 - 60%	85 – 102 Bpm / 6	2 minutes
60 - 70%	102 – 119 Bpm / 7	2 minutes
70 - 80%	119 – 136 Bpm / 8	2 minutes
80 - 90%	136 – 153 Bpm / 9	1 - 2 minutes
70 - 80%	119 – 136 Bpm / 8	2 minutes
60 - 70%	102 – 119 Bpm / 7	2 minutes
50 - 60%	85 – 102 Bpm / 6	2 minutes
5 minute cool down		

Steady State Training

You will be using this type of training throughout a large percentage of your program, working at a comfortable intensity of around 50% - 70% of your maximum heart rate or between 5 – 7 on the RPE scale.

This type of training requires that you don't change the speed at which you run at all, you simply maintain a comfortable pace throughout. Using this type of training should still allow you to be able to talk and the intensity should feel 'comfortable.'

Power Walking

When power walking, the aim is to walk at speed and maintain this for some time. You will need to involve your arms, lean forwards, and really stride out. Try to pull in your abdominal muscles and breathe regularly and rhythmically. This should feel hard and at a pace you would walk at if you were running late for an appointment.

Walk/Run

Whenever you see this in the program, it means that you should run as far as you can and then walk until you feel recovered enough to run again. Obviously aim to run as much as possible, but don't push yourself too far at this stage. Try to do more each time. If you are using a particular route, try to reach given points such as a certain house, landmark, etc., and the next time you run it again, try to go a bit further.

Tempo Run

This is basically a running pace that is a little faster than normal steady state training pace, or one that you can run and still hold a conversation comfortably, RPE 5-7 and in the heart rate zone 50 – 70%.

A tempo run requires you to run at a higher intensity so you can no longer hold a full conversation, instead you are only able to say just a few words before having to take a breath. Tempo pace would be RPE 7-8 and heart rate zone 70-80%.

The good thing about tempo running is that it prepares your body for running at a faster pace, without the stops and starts you will have when you practice interval training and other techniques. If you just kept running at the same pace all the time, any occasions when you needed to run any faster would quickly take their toll on your body.

The Structure of a Session

Each session should be a little varied and progressive. In other words, you should do more than the last time you did the same session.

Each workout needs to start with a graduated warm up; usually 5 minutes of brisk walking or a very gentle jog is enough. The aim here is to raise the temperature of the muscles, increase the work rate of the heart, and warm up the lungs.

Always finish off each workout with a 5-minute cool down. Again, walking is good here followed by the stretches as outlined in chapter 6.

On Land, Sea, or Air?

You should run on whatever surface you feel comfortable on, whether that be grass, sand, road, or rugged terrain.

A certain amount of training should be done on different surfaces, to allow for adaptations in your balance and stabilising and supporting muscles and tendons, etc. Just running many, many miles on the road can be a huge challenge for your bones and joints.

If you know the route of the 5k race you will be doing, then you should aim to mimic this as much as possible in your training sessions.

Flexibility and Stretching for Runners

The more you exercise and run, the more prone you become to muscular imbalances. The lower back, calves, and hamstrings can become tight and inflexible while the shins, quadriceps, and stomach muscles may actually get weaker in comparison. Stretching will help to counteract this.

Flexibility is one the most often overlooked parts of health and fitness. Flexibility naturally diminishes with age but also as you start to increase your distances you will notice that your muscles seem to be getting a little tighter.

Runners need to primarily concentrate on stretching off the muscles of the legs and lower back in order to return them to their pre-exercise length.

Always warm the muscles up first before stretching by walking briskly or gentle jogging for 5 minutes. This helps to increase heat in the area, making the muscles more pliable and less likely to tear if stretched too vigorously. This means if you want to stretch before exercise, you should do so after an initial warm up period.

Stretching before exercise is not necessary, but it certainly won't hurt if you choose to. The important time to stretch is after exercise. During exercise the muscles contract repeatedly, leading to slightly shorter and tighter muscles, which need help to be lengthened and stretched out. This is where stretching is very beneficial as it returns the muscles to their pre-exercise state.

Regular stretching offers the following benefits:

• Helps prevent muscular aches, pains, and cramping

- Reduces the possibility of muscular soreness over the following days
- Decreases the possibility of suffering mechanical muscular injuries
- Increases the muscles' ability to lengthen and stretch during exercise
- Improves the muscles' ability to work faster, harder, and more efficiently
- Allows you to safely improve stride length
- Improves overall posture and running technique

You should use static stretching instead of ballistic stretching to safely lengthen your muscles and improve flexibility.

Ballistic Stretching

Ballistic stretching is a very advanced form of stretching used to aggressively improve the muscles' ability to lengthen. It is not advisable to attempt this unsupervised and without sufficient experience or physiological knowledge.

During ballistic stretching, you bounce into the stretch in an attempt to beat the stretch reflex (the sensation or sharp pain you receive that stops you from going too far when trying to increase the length or duration of a stretch).

Static Stretching

Static stretching involves taking the muscle to the point of its greatest range of motion, without overextending it. Done correctly, you should get a slight feeling of tightness or mild discomfort at about 6 or 7 on the RPE scale. This should not be a sharp or shooting pain; that would indicate that you are stretching too far and should ease back a little. This sharp pain is called the stretch reflex and its job is to ensure that you don't take the muscles further in to a stretch than they are comfortably able to go. The way we improve flexibility is by working with the stretch reflex which is known as developmental stretching. You can do this as follows:

• Get into a stretch position and take the muscle to a point where you can feel a mild discomfort, just a little further back from where you felt a sharper pain (the stretch reflex).
• Wait for approximately 15 – 20 seconds without pushing any further until the discomfort becomes milder and then ease slowly further into the stretch until you again feel the stretch reflex. Ease back a little from here and hold this position.
• This can be repeated a few times, but ideally you should move on to another muscle after a minute to avoid stressing the muscle too far.

When stretching after running you need to focus on all the main muscles groups you've used in your session. These are:

Quadriceps – the muscles that run down the front of your thighs, crossing the knee and hip joints
Hamstrings – the muscles down the back of the legs
Adductors – the muscles on the inside of the thighs at the top of the legs
Hip Flexors – the muscles at the top and front of the thighs
Gluteus Maximus – the muscles of the buttocks
Gastrocnemius – the longest muscle in the calves just below the knee
Soleus – the shorter muscle of the calves just above the ankle

The following advice should be adhered to when stretching:

• Do not overextend the muscles.

- You should feel very minimal tightness/discomfort (but not pain).
- Hold and control the stretch for at least 15 - 30 seconds.
- Stretch all the major leg muscle groups as listed above.
- Stretch uniformly (after stretching one leg, stretch the other).
- Don't overstretch an injured area as this may cause additional damage.
- Never bounce when stretching as this can increase your chances of suffering an injury!

Always include stretching after a run; make it part of the training and cool down process, get into the habit. Your legs will be the most receptive to the benefits of stretching straight after you run. Stretch gently and slowly and while your muscles are still warm.

If your flexibility is quite poor, a regular program of stretching will help to rectify the problem. Stretching every day is a good idea, but always after you have warmed the muscles up first.

Roadside Stretches

Gastrocnemius (upper calf) Stretch

● Stand tall with one leg in front of the other, hands flat and at shoulder height against a wall

● Keep your hips facing the wall with the rear leg and spine in a straight line and bend your front leg

● Push against the wall and press the back heel into the ground, there shouldn't be any pressure on the front foot

● You should feel the stretch in the calf of the straight leg

● Repeat with the other leg

Soleus (lower calf) Stretch

- Standing as above, bring your back foot in closer to the wall and bend the bent leg a little more
- Keep both feet flat on the floor, you should feel a stretch in your lower calf of the back leg
- Leaning towards the wall intensifies the stretch
- There should be little pressure on the front foot
- Repeat with the other leg

Standing Quadriceps (front of thigh) Stretch

- Lean against a wall and bend your right knee, grasping the right foot with your right hand behind you
- Lift your foot backwards until your heel is as close as possible to the buttocks, without touching
- Flex your foot and keep your body straight
- Push the hips a little further forward if you can't feel the stretch down the front of the thighs
- Repeat with the other leg

Hamstring (back of thigh) Stretch

- Stand with your left foot placed flat on the ground in front of you and keep your extended leg straight
- Bend the right thigh, stick your bottom out and place your hands on your bent leg for support
- Lean forwards into your straight leg, pushing your bottom out, then straighten up your upper body until you can feel a stretch down the back of the straight leg
- Repeat with the other leg

Hip Flexor (front of upper thigh) Stretch

- Take a long lunge forward
- Keep your hips square and your upper body vertical
- Place your hands on your front thigh
- Dip your back knee towards the ground until you feel a stretch down the back thigh, high up towards the top of your leg
- Repeat with the other leg

Adductor (inner thigh) Stretch

- Stand tall with both feet pointing forwards, approximately two shoulders width apart
- Bend the right leg, place both hands on the bent thigh and lower the body towards the ground, keeping the left leg straight
- Keep your back straight and chest out
- You should feel this stretch high up the leg on the inside just below the groin of the straight leg
- Repeat with the other leg

Standing Glute (buttocks) Stretch

- Lean with your back against a wall for support
- Take hold of your right leg with both arms around the calf
- Pull in towards the chest until you can feel a stretch down the back of the right buttock
- Repeat with the other leg

Standing Tibialis Stretch

- Stand with a hip width foot spacing and your knees slightly bent
- Bend your right knee and grasp the toes of your right foot with your right hand, move your right knee forward
- Pull up on your toes forcing the top of your foot downwards
- You should feel this stretch down the front of the right shin
- Place one hand against a wall for balance if necessary
- Repeat with the other leg

Combined Stretches

The stretching techniques below allow you to stretch a number of muscles at the same time which means you can stretch much quicker. These can be done at home where you can use either a mat or towel to sit on.

Lying Quadriceps and Tibialis Stretch

- Sit down on to the floor on your bent knees with your buttocks on top of your feet
- Make sure the tops of your feet are flat on the floor with your toes pointing backwards
- Gently lean backwards as far as you can comfortably go until you can feel the stretch down the front of the thighs and the shins

Hamstring and Adductor Stretch

- Sit on the ground with both legs straight out in front of you
- Bend the left leg and place the sole of the left foot alongside the knee of the right leg
- Allow the right leg to lie relaxed on the ground and bend forward, keeping the back straight
- You should feel the stretch down the back of the left leg and inside of the right upper thigh
- Repeat with the other leg

Simultaneous Gastrocnemius Stretch

- Using a wall for support, place both hands against it and take a wide stride backwards
- Keep both heels flat on the floor
- Lean forwards keeping your back and legs straight
- You should feel this stretch in both calves at the same time

Gluteus and Lower Back Stretch

- Lying on the floor on your back
- Wrap both arms around the front of the shins and pull the thighs in towards the body
- Round your spine and hold that position
- You should be feeling this stretch on the lower back and around the buttocks

Final Thoughts

- Don't stretch cold muscles. It is far better to stretch after a run than before one.
- Do stretch lightly before doing any speed training, after a 5–10 minute warm up.
- Ease into your stretches gently, don't bounce or force them.
- After a run, hold each stretch for 30 seconds and repeat once or twice on each leg.

All About Injuries

Perhaps the biggest challenge to any beginner starting a running program is not completing the actual race but making it to race day without any serious or niggling injuries.

Unfortunately, the truth is that most runners will pick up an injury of some sort at one time or another throughout their training. The causes of these injuries can be wide and varied, but almost all involve the lower body and many of them can be avoided if the correct technique, training plan, and running shoes have been chosen.

The way you run can dictate your chances of suffering from injuries because most running injuries are caused by muscle tightness, weakness, or imbalances. These also make your running form less efficient and more stressful on the joints.

Usually, the landing part of your stride is the cause of injuries you may suffer from because of the impact transmitted throughout the body with each step which can be so great that any slight flaws in your running style are magnified enormously.

Injuries can be classified into 2 main groups: acute or chronic. Acute running injuries can usually be identified the moment they have been caused. For example, a bone may break during a fall or a muscle may tear while training. Treatment of this type of injury usually requires rest, meaning you will not be aggravating the damaged area and therefore recovery can be quite rapid.

Chronic injuries develop over time and can be difficult to heal. Because they are not as severe in nature, many runners continue through them, even though their training may have to be reduced slightly. This can often lead to quite serious long-term problems.

Common Running Injuries

Shin Splints

This is a generic term for pain at the front of the shins. It actually encompasses a range of different problems that can occur at the shin bone itself, from muscle tightness, nerve pain to stress. A change in running technique, frequency, or running surface are all known triggers.

Muscle Tears

Muscle tears aren't a common injury that runners suffer because they don't need to make sudden explosive or quick twisting movements.

Ligament Tears

Ligament tears can be a problem with runners, especially in the ankles or knees, and are usually caused by a misplaced foot.

Ilio-Tibial Band Syndrome (ITB syndrome)

The ilio-tibial band is a muscle down the outside of the leg. After this becomes larger through constant use, it can rub against a piece of bone/fatpad just above the knee. There are several factors which could bring on this type of knee pain including muscular imbalance, weakness, poor leg alignment, and a change in running style.

Achilles Tendonitis

This is perhaps the most common injury suffered by runners and accounts for over 20% of all running injuries. The Achilles tendon is located at the back of the heel. Causes of pain can be from a number of sources. Fatigue in the calf muscle, change in running technique, nerve damage, and poor circulation are all known triggers.

Plantar Fasciitis

This is a pain in the middle of the sole of foot and is caused by an abnormal landing foot position or calf muscles that are too tight. Choosing the right footwear can make a huge difference to this problem.

Piriformis Syndrome

The piriformis is a deep muscle of the buttocks. This muscle stabilizes the body during training. The muscle can go into spasm or become inflamed. When it does this, because of its close proximity to the sciatic nerve, this can press against the nerve, causing pain down the leg and buttocks. Stretching the muscle is usually considered to be the best preventative treatment.

Stress Fracture

The most common acute injury experienced while training for a marathon is a stress fracture. A stress fracture is an incomplete fracture of a bone caused by repeated stress (for example constant pounding of the foot on a pavement). Rest is the only option for complete healing of a stress fracture.

Patello-femoral joint pain (PFJP)

Patello-femoral joint pain is one of the top five problems runners can suffer from. The reason for this is that the patella bone (kneecap) and surrounding tissues can cause the problem. The shape or position of the patella may be abnormal or there may be damage to the surrounding tissues around it. Running gait and landing foot position are common causes of PFJP. Changes in frequency, duration, or intensity of training are the most common triggers for this complaint.

Foot pain

Foot pain is a very common runner's complaint which can be caused by stress fractures, plantar fasciitis, and blisters. Pain around the feet is by far the most common complaint in runners. Treatment depends on the problem, but once again, look for and then treat that trigger to ensure it doesn't happen again.

Runner's Knee

This is a wearing away of the back of the kneecap during your training for a 5k, causing pain in the knee. It primarily occurs because of an imbalance between the hamstrings and quadriceps muscles or shoes that do not give the right type of support.

Be cautious throughout your training. Some of these injuries can end your training for a long time.

Less Serious Injuries

Blisters

Many people suffer from blisters needlessly; they are a constant threat for runners, but they can be avoided. By selecting specialist running socks, applying petroleum jelly to the feet prior to running, and wearing in new trainers gradually you should be able to avoid this runner's blight.

Damage to the toenails

The constant impact and movement of your feet to the front of your trainers are the usual causes of this complaint. To avoid this make sure that your trainers are a good fit. (See section on selecting the correct footwear.)

Runner's nipple

This problem manifests itself through the constant friction of clothing over the nipple area because of repeated rubbing which can cause inflammation and bleeding of the nipple. To avoid this either cover the nipples in petroleum jelly or cover using a sticking plaster.

Use Body Glide, Skin Lube, Lanacane, Vaseline or similar products (on feet, under arms, between thighs, on and around nipples, etc.) to eliminate the chances of suffering from chafing and blisters.

Cramp

Muscle cramping is when a muscle begins to spasm and contracts intensely. The exact causes of muscle cramps are often debated but the most likely reasons are dehydration, tired and shortened muscles, or an imbalance of electrolytes (mineral salts within the blood). By regularly stretching, drinking plenty of water, and maintaining a normal balance of electrolytes, possibly through vitamin and mineral supplementation, you should be able to avoid this problem.

Stitches

A stitch is a deep throbbing pain felt in the abdominal area which often causes sufferers to stop training. There is no single definite answer for the cause or treatment of a stitch; the most popular theory is that they are caused by either drinking too much or eating a meal too near to running as it's this extra 'bounce' from the weight of food and drink in the stomach that causes a ligament which connects the stomach to the rib cage to go in to spasm.

Whenever you move your body, blood flow gets diverted to the working muscles instead or the internal organs. This means If you have just had a meal then there is not enough blood being sent to the digestive system to digest food which could also cause stomach problems.

Another theory is the diaphragm (the muscle that assists in breathing) can go into spasm due to fatigue. If you do get a stitch, try to hold your stomach in either by contracting the muscles or placing your hands over the area and squeezing, breathe using shallow breaths, slow down, and reduce the bounce in your stride. If none of these work, you may need to stop for a couple of minutes for it to wear off.

Treating Injuries

If you feel an increase in pain after an injury, you should stop because running through this pain will only slow down the recovery process or even make the injury more serious. A more sinister outcome is that by continuing to run and subconsciously protecting the injury by altering your natural running style, a secondary injury may develop.

For any muscular tears, the usual form of action is abbreviated into the acronym RICE: -

REST – Don't train for at least 24 – 28 hours; depending on the severity of the tear, try not to use it at all for the immediate preceding hours.

ICE – Apply a bag of ice or frozen peas to the damaged area. This helps to constrict the capillaries which can reduce muscle bleeding.

COMPRESSION – Apply pressure to the area using a bandage or tying something around it. This can reduce swelling and bleeding.

ELEVATION – The idea behind this is to raise the damaged area above the heart to reduce blood flow, thereby lessening bleeding and speeding up the healing process.

Any injury lasting more than a couple of weeks, or one that gets worse with subsequent runs, will require medical attention. Make an appointment to see a professional. It is important to see the right person as injuries can be misdiagnosed at times, which usually leads to much longer recovery times.

Physiotherapists, sports therapists, chiropractors, massage therapists, and osteopaths are all experts that could be considered. Always check they hold current qualifications and if possible have been recommended to you by someone you know personally. Ask them to diagnose the problem and to give you advice as how to train, rest, and repair the area. Also, ask how long the injury could take to heal and how many visits you might need to make.

How to Prevent Injuries

By following the instructions in this guide and increasing your distances very gradually you should be able to avoid and prevent the most common of these injuries. Above all else, always listen to what your body is telling you. If you feel the first signs of something wrong, don't simply run through it. Stop to investigate it further. Unfortunately, the sad truth is that many runners cause themselves serious long-term injury by working through seemingly small pains because of an unwillingness to stop or slow down.

The following points should give you an overview of the best ways to avoid suffering from injuries:

• Make slow and gradual changes when increasing the distance you run.
• Make sure to alternate your training days and always take rest days.
• Spend some time and money choosing the right type of footwear for your particular running style.
• Always listen to your body.
• Make sure you stretch regularly both before and after your training.

- Include a thorough and gradual warm up which includes a gentle increase in the heart rate, warmth of the muscles, then mobilizing the joints and relevant stretches.
- Drink plenty of fluids daily.
- Avoid overtraining.
- Try to train on a variety of running surfaces. Road, grass, and dirt tracks are ideal for strengthening the deeper muscles of the lower body. However, you should ease into different surfaces gradually; for example, don't simply decide one day that you are going to run a long distance on an unusual surface. Instead, try much shorter runs at first and build up from there.
- If in doubt, consult your physiotherapist or doctor.

The Running Programs

The goal of running a 5k in a certain number of weeks is very achievable within reason, but everyone has a different starting point and also a different potential for becoming fitter and improving their own endurance levels.

Judge and compare yourself only against yourself. If you are regularly progressing and improving, you are on the right track. If you have been sticking to your chosen training program and working towards your SMART goals you will be fine.

I really recommend booking a place on your first 5k race as soon as you have started your training and you're sure that it is something you would like to continue with. Once you have decided that you enjoy running then you are ready to seriously start your training.

All the programs are at the back of this manual, but first things first: we need to decide the appropriate starting point for you. Select from one of the following programs based on your current fitness levels and your expectations of what you would like to achieve during the race – to walk it, to just complete without stopping, or to run in a certain time frame.

If you're a complete beginner and can't run further than the end of your street and then need to sit down for 10 minutes to recover, you will need to follow "Program 1 - Training to Walk a 5K:

If your aim is to simply complete a 5k without stopping then you should look at one of two options – "Program 2 - Beginner to 5k" or "Program 3 - Run a Faster 5k"

Finally, if you are already quite fit and can manage running a mile on the flat without too much difficulty, a regular exerciser and very competitive and motivated, then you should use "Program 4 – New World Record!" during which you will be aiming to run your fastest possible time.

Be honest with yourself. Overestimating your abilities at the start could lead to suffering injuries as your body hasn't had the chance to acclimatise itself to the new stresses and strains you are placing it under.

It is extremely important not to try and rush the training process or attempt to force your body to change too quickly as this is the fastest way to pick up injuries and over-train, which can lead to tiredness, lethargy, depression, loss of appetite, and illness.

When you start each training session, do bear in mind that the first 10 -15 minutes are often the most awkward and uncomfortable. After this point there will be a small rise in body temperature (approximately one degree) and the blood will start to flow faster to the working muscles. When you reach this point, you will begin sweating slightly as your body begins its cooling down process. This is often referred to as your 'second wind.'

Start off slowly until you reach this point so that you are working with your body instead of against it.

Please remember these programs aren't set in stone; be flexible to some degree if you need to. There will occasionally be times when you can't manage to do your workout through work or family commitments, illness, injury, or just general tiredness. Don't beat yourself up over it, simply try to fit it in another time.

For the sake of planning I have written the programs to suit particular days, allowing for rest days also. You would be unusually lucky if you could perform your sessions exactly as I have written them, although with some organization, doing sessions in the morning before work, at lunchtime, or later in the evenings should be looked at carefully.

If you do have to reorganize sessions, try to do so in advance and write them down, for example at the beginning of the week. As much as possible, try to allow rest days in between workout days.

Sundays have been designated as the day when you do your longer runs, simply because this is usually a time when most people can spare some time consistently.

You will notice on some of the programs there are a number of references to certain types of training. These have been covered in detail in the section on Advanced Training Techniques.

DIY Training Program

If you want to create your own program around your lifestyle, work, family, etc. then you should include the following aspects: -

● Plan to do your longest run at the weekend; these should be slow with the mileage gradually increasing each week.
● Include a shorter run most weeks.
● Include some tempo running but for shorter distances.
● Add some hill, interval, sprint, pyramid and Fartlek training into your program to add extra training stimulus and variety.
● Always allow yourself at least 3 days rest each week.
● Reduce your weekly mileage when adding speed work.
● Alternate easy days with hard training days.
● Use cross training for variety and to improve your aerobic endurance.
● Do not increase your weekly mileage by more than 10% each week. Doing so greatly increases the chances of incurring an injury.

Try Something a Little Different

Fitness is definitely relative to the sport or activity that you do the most of and your body will adapt specifically to this stimulation and the way it has been trained. To get better at something you need to practice that particular activity. But that isn't to say that you shouldn't perform other forms of exercise that will compliment your training.

For example, yoga is a very good way to lengthen tight muscles and help you to control and focus on your breathing technique.

Strengthening your muscles by using resistance training will also help your performance enormously; just beware of hitting the weights too hard, especially on your legs. Otherwise you won't be able to walk for a week, let alone run!

Taking Weeks Off

Yes, you read that right, you should and absolutely must take some time off from running every so often. I recommend that you do so when you have completed your first 5k race. You don't have to do absolutely nothing, although you can if you want to.

Instead go swimming a couple of times or out for a cycle ride. Whatever you choose to do, the idea is to return to training refreshed and ready to move on again. It's a chance for your body to recover from any aches and pains that may have accumulated during the last phase of your training.

PROGRAM 1 – Training to Walk a 5K

Who is it For?

This program is ideally suited to the following people:

- Anyone who is new to fitness or currently inactive.
- Anyone who is overweight.
- Anyone who is trying to lose weight.
- Anyone who is recovering from injury.
- Any elderly or very young exercisers.

Workout Goals

To successfully complete a 5k race by walking all the way without stopping.

Workout Duration

The program is based over 6 weeks.

Specific Workout Notes and Guidelines

When embarking on any new form of exercise which involves the repetitive movement of certain joints over extended periods of time such as walking, it is vital that you ensure that the footwear you select is appropriate for your needs.

Running shoes are perfect for road or track walking etc but if you intend to do any of your training off road using tracks, paths, over grass, sand, or mud, it will be a good investment to spend some extra money on a good pair of walking boots. The reason for this is that they have a much higher support around the ankle which helps to protect and stabilise the joint against slight deviations in footfall and walking surfaces.

Start off slowly at first. While your aim may be to just walk a 5k race without resting, the very fact that you have selected this option means that your starting point is still very far from being able to achieve this goal.

The risks of suffering from injuries due to your training are far less likely than if you were training to run the race, so you won't need to take as much rest in between workouts. But if you are quite overweight, then the risk to your knees, lower back, and ankles is still quite considerable, so you will need to listen to your body and be aware of any aches, pains, and niggles you may feel.

During your sessions an aching in the muscles is to be expected, especially if you are walking up a gradient or using bursts of speed throughout your training. In fact, we actually want this type of reaction from the body.

What we don't want is any sharp or shooting pains, so if you feel any of these, stop immediately to investigate the problem further.

Unless specified, select routes for your sessions that contain no hills or just slight gradients for your first few walks or any of the gentle walks listed in the program.

WEEKS	MONDAY	TUESDAY	WEDNESDAY	THURSDAY	FRIDAY	SATURDAY	SUNDAY
1	Gentle walk 10 minutes	REST	Gentle Walk 2 x 10 minutes	REST	Gentle Walk 20 minutes	REST	Gentle Walk 1 mile/1.6km
2	Cross Training 15 minutes	REST	Gentle Walk 2 x 15 minutes	REST	Hill Walk 10 minutes	REST	Walk 1½ miles/2.4km
3	Cross Training 20 minutes	REST	Gentle Walk 2 x 20 minutes	REST	Interval Training 25 minutes	REST	Walk 2 miles/3.2km
4	Cross Training 30 minutes	REST	Walk 30 minutes	REST	Hill Walk 15 minutes	REST	Gentle Walk 2½ miles/4km
5	Cross Training 35 minutes	REST	Power Walk 35 minutes	REST	Interval Training 30 minutes	REST	Walk 3 miles/4.8km
6	Cross Training 45 minutes	REST	Walk 45 minutes	REST	Hill Walk 30 minutes	REST	Brisk Walk 3½ miles/5.6km

Gentle Walk

A gentle walk is meant to be performed at a comfortable pace, using the RPE scale, around 5 or 6/10 is ideal; do not push yourself too hard during these sessions. In the program where the gentle walk is written as '2 x 10 minutes,' for example, this means that you should perform two short walks at different times of the day, not immediately after each other.

Power Walk

This is brisk walking at a fast pace, trying to maintain a constant speed. You should start to sweat slightly and your breathing should be constantly elevated. A score of 6 or 7/10 on the RPE scale is the perfect level of intensity for you.

Cross Training

This section of the program is meant to provide aerobic training to improve the strength and endurance of the heart and lungs at the same time as resting the muscles and joints used during walking. I recommend swimming, cycling, fitness DVDs, circuit training, etc. Basically, anything which doesn't use the same mechanics as walking.

Hill Walk

Select any hills or inclines nearby to perform this session on. The aim during these workouts is build up strength in the leg muscles and the heart and lungs. You should spend the allotted time actually walking up the hill, so the total time for a session wouldn't include the amount of time you spent walking downhill for example. If you don't have access to any hills, try using an inclinable treadmill or if you aren't able to use one, you can power walk instead.

Interval Training

There are two interval sessions in this program and for these you will use three different levels of intensity and speed: gentle walking, brisk walking, and power walking. You can either choose to use landmarks for your intervals such as lamp posts or markers in the road, or alternatively use a stopwatch to time one-minute intervals at each speed.

Sunday Sessions

Once a week you will need to develop your endurance by performing some longer walks so that you build up to race day distance. You can of course choose any day to do this, but to suit the program and fit in rest days I have structured Sundays as this day.

If you live in or near the area of the race you have selected to run then you can plan your routes to have similar hills or inclines, and this way you will be perfectly prepared for the race.

PROGRAM 2 – Beginner to 5K

Who is it For?

This program is ideally suited to the following people:

- Beginners who are new to running.
- Anyone who is looking for a mini challenge to achieve.
- Anyone who is trying to lose weight.
- Anyone who has no injuries or niggles.

Workout Goals

To successfully complete a 5k race by running all the way without stopping.

Workout Duration

The program is based over 8 weeks.

Specific Workout Notes and Guidelines

The important point to remember here is not to get impatient.

Running any distance when you are not used to doing so places a large amount of stress on the body, especially the joints. For that reason, this program introduces small and manageable amounts of gentle running to begin with which then increase over the duration of the 8 weeks.

You will notice that I ask you to attempt one long run each week, but by this I mean that I simply want you to run as far as you can without stopping. This session then becomes your benchmark for future runs, and you will aim to improve each subsequent time you attempt it. Doing this weekly allows you to realistically assess your progress.

Each session should begin with a warmup such as a brisk walk or at the latter stages of the program a very gentle jog, followed by leg stretches.

The vital part of this program is to be consistent in your training. When you are trying to build a level of fitness from being completely inactive, your progress will be compromised if you don't train regularly; a stop-start mentality will only serve to frustrate and de-motivate you, so unless you have an injury or are physically ill, you really do need to commit to training on the days shown in your program.

One final point that you need to be aware of so you can spot it and react accordingly is that you may feel achy and stiff when you first start your running regime, it is quite normal to feel like this and the good news is that it only lasts a few sessions, although many of your workouts could well begin this way until you have properly loosened up.

WEEKS	MONDAY	TUESDAY	WEDNESDAY	THURSDAY	FRIDAY	SATURDAY	SUNDAY
1	Walk 20 minutes	REST	Walk/Run 20 minutes	REST	Gentle Walk 45 minutes	REST	Walk/Run 1 mile
2	Cross Training 15 minutes	REST	Walk 25 minutes	REST	Walk/Run 30 minutes	REST	Walk/Run 1 mile
3	Cross Training 20 minutes	REST	Walk 30 minutes	REST	Interval Training 25 minutes	REST	Walk/Run 1½ miles
4	Cross Training 30 minutes	REST	Walk 35 minutes	REST	Walk/Power Walk 60 minutes	REST	Run 1½ miles
5	Cross Training 35 minutes	REST	Power Walk 30 minutes	REST	Run 1½ miles	REST	Run 2 miles
6	Cross Training 45 minutes	REST	Power Walk 35 minutes	REST	Run 2 miles	REST	Run 2 miles
7	Cross Training 50 minutes	REST	Walk/Run 2 miles	REST	Pyramid Training 30 minutes	REST	Run 2½ miles
8	Cross Training 60 minutes	REST	Walk/Run 3 miles	REST	Interval Training 30 minutes	REST	Run 3 miles

Walk/Power Walk or Walk/Run

During these sessions you will choose set points in the distance to power walk or run to. There shouldn't be any real structure, simply increase your speed when you feel able to. Run as much as you can but don't overdo it or push it too far, and just walk in between.

Power Walk

You will be brisk walking at a fast pace, maintaining a constant speed. You may start sweating slightly and your breathing should be constantly elevated. A score of 6 or 7/10 on the RPE scale is the perfect level of intensity for you.

Cross Training

This section of the program is meant to provide aerobic training to improve the strength and endurance of the heart and lungs whilst resting the muscles and joints used during your runs. I suggest swimming, cycling, fitness DVDs, circuit training, etc. Basically, anything which challenges the body differently than running.

Walk

You should aim to walk at your normal or natural pace for these sessions, not a brisk speed but not a saunter either. Where possible use a variety of terrains as this helps to provide stimulus for your muscles to become stronger at the same time as helping to improve the strength and stability of the ankles, knees, and lower back.

Interval Training

You will use three different levels of intensity and speed for these sessions: walking, slow jogging, and running. You can either choose to use landmarks for your intervals such as lamp posts or markers in the road, or alternatively use a stopwatch to time one-minute intervals at each speed.

Pyramid Training

Choose relatively flat terrain for this session and see notes for further details.

Run

Don't set off too fast; the secret to running as a beginner is to slow your pace right down. Many new runners set off too fast and have to stop prematurely due to fatigue. Ideally, I want you to be able to run a set distance, no matter how fast; thereafter you can increase your speeds and improve your running times. On the RPE scale you would be aiming for a 6/10. If you can't run for any distance without the effort feeling harder than this, then slow your speed down or build up your power walking speed instead.

Sunday Sessions

Once a week you will need to develop your endurance by performing some actual runs so that you build up to race day distance. You can of course choose any day to do this, but to suit the program and fit in with rest days I have structured Sundays as this day.

PROGRAM 3 – Run a Faster 5K

Who is it For?

This program is ideally suited to the following people:

- Anyone who has run a 5k in the past and wants to run one faster.
- Anyone who wants to complete a 5k in under 30 minutes.
- Anyone who can run for 5 minutes without stopping.
- Anyone who is competitive.
- Anyone who is a regular exerciser with a good level of fitness.

Workout Goals

To successfully complete a 5k in under 30 minutes without stopping.

Workout Duration

The program is based over 6 weeks.

Specific Workout Notes and Guidelines

This program is all about pushing your fitness levels further throughout the course of the 6 weeks. We will be using quite a few advanced training techniques in order to improve the ability of your heart and lungs to take in and distribute the oxygen to the working muscles much more efficiently.

These advanced training techniques will also quickly build in strength and endurance in the legs so you can keep going for longer without fatigue and lactic acid build up in the muscles forcing you to stop.

During this program your rest days are vital. Always leave one day recovery in between workouts especially after the higher intensity sessions.

Because we are working towards a specific finishing time, we need to monitor your pace at regular intervals. For this reason, you will perform a timed mile each week. This can be measured in a number of ways, firstly by using a measured mile which you can gauge by driving the route in your car.

Secondly, you can work out your route by visiting one of these websites:
http://www.walkjogrun.net
http://www.mapmyrun.com

Finally, you can get hold of a pedometer or a wristwatch GPS tracking device which will be able to measure your route exactly.

To complete a 5k in under 30 minutes you need to run at a pace of 9.5 mins/mile.
To complete a 5k in under 28 minutes you need to run at a pace of 9 mins/mile.
To complete a 5k in under 25 minutes you need to run at a pace of 8 mins/mile.

During the race you will need to monitor your pace and either increase or decrease the speed you are running accordingly so you finish in your ideal time. Bear in mind that this program is designed not to simply complete the race, but to do so in a respectable time and our target throughout Program 3 is to complete the race in under 30 minutes.

WEEKS	MONDAY	TUESDAY	WEDNESDAY	THURSDAY	FRIDAY	SATURDAY	SUNDAY
1	Walk/Run 20 minutes	REST	Power Walk 20 minutes	REST	Cross Training 30 minutes	REST	Timed Mile + 1 mile extra
2	Cross Training 15 minutes	REST	Timed Mile 1 mile	REST	Walk/Run 45 minutes	REST	Walk/Run 2 miles
3	Cross Training 20 minutes	REST	Power Walk 30 minutes	REST	Interval Training 25 minutes	REST	2 Timed Miles + 2 miles extra
4	Cross Training 30 minutes	REST	Interval Training 30 minutes	REST	Hill Reps 20 minutes	REST	Race Distance Timed – 3 miles
5	Cross Training 35 minutes	REST	Pyramid Training 30 minutes	REST	Run 1½ miles	REST	Timed Mile + Run 2 miles
6	Cross Training 45 minutes	REST	Fartlek Training 30 minutes	REST	Run 2 miles	REST	Timed Mile + Run 3 miles

Gentle Walk

A gentle walk is meant to be performed at a comfortable pace, using the RPE scale, around 5 or 6/10 is ideal; do not push yourself too hard during these sessions.

Walk

You should aim to walk at your normal or natural pace for these sessions, not a brisk speed but not a saunter either. Where possible use a variety of terrains as this helps to provide stimulus for your muscles to become stronger at the same time as helping to improve the strength and stability of the ankles, knees, and lower back.

Walk/Power Walk or Walk/Run

During these sessions you will choose set points in the distance to power walk or run to. There shouldn't be any real structure to this, simply increase your speed when you feel able to. Run as much as you can, but don't overdo it or push it too far.

Power Walk

You will be brisk walking at a fast pace, maintaining a constant speed. You may start sweating slightly and your breathing should be constantly elevated. A score of 6 or 7/10 on the RPE scale is the perfect level of intensity for you during these walks.

Cross Training

This section of the program is meant to provide aerobic training to improve the strength and endurance of the heart and lungs whilst resting the muscles and joints used during your runs. I suggest swimming, cycling, fitness DVDs, circuit training, etc. Basically, anything which challenges the body differently than running.

Interval Training

You will use three different levels of intensity and speed for these sessions: walking, slow jogging, and running. You can either choose to use landmarks for your intervals such as lamp posts or markers in the road, or alternatively use a stopwatch to time one-minute intervals at each speed.

Pyramid Training

Choose relatively flat terrain for this session and see detailed notes for further details.

Run

Don't set off too fast; the secret to running as a beginner is to slow your pace right down. Many new runners set off too fast and have to stop prematurely due to fatigue. Ideally, I want you to be able to run a set distance, no matter how fast; thereafter you can increase your speeds and improve your running times. On the RPE scale you would be aiming for a 6/10. If you can't run for any distance without the effort feeling harder than this, then slow your speed down or build up your power walking speed instead.

Sunday Sessions

Once a week you will need to develop your endurance by performing some longer runs and building up to race day distance. You can of course choose any day to do this, but to suit the program and fit in with rest days I have structured Sundays as this day.

You will also notice that this is the day you will perform your timed mile. The reason behind this is to ensure that you are achieving the speeds you need to reach in order to complete the race in your desired finishing time.

Hill Reps

Choose the steepest incline you can find within an easy to reach distance from your home. Ideally the hill you choose should be enough of a challenge so that you reach a point where you need to stop running up it because of fatigue in the legs and an unsustainably high breathing rate. If the hill is too steep you will gain the same benefits and improvements by power walking up it instead.

Following this program, you should be aiming to spend the allotted time actually running or power walking up the hill. Do not include your descent in the overall time you allow for this session. This may well mean running the same section of the hill a number of times, which is fine. We are aiming to build in power to the legs and endurance and improve your anaerobic threshold.

Fartlek Training

In phase 3 you will attempt a full 30 minute Fartlek training. For full details see the section in Advanced Training Techniques. Specifically for this session, you are aiming to run the full workout and intersperse this with bursts of faster running or any inclines. You will simply be changing speed when you feel able to. If you feel tired slow down and if you feel fine, increase your speed.

Timed Mile +

This session is meant to be a monitoring session, where you will time a mile and aim to run at a pace that will allow you to complete the race in your desired time. When you have completed your timed mile, either stop for a few minutes to catch your breath or continue until you complete the desired distance. Timed mile + 2 miles, means you run for a mile whilst timing yourself and then go on to complete a further 2 miles, ideally running.

PROGRAM 4 – New World Record!

Who is it For?

This program is ideally suited to the following people:

- Anyone who has run a few 5ks in the past and wants to run one faster.
- Anyone who wants to complete a 5k in their fastest time possible.
- Anyone who can run for 30 minutes comfortably without stopping.
- Anyone who is very competitive.
- Anyone who is a regular exerciser with a good level of fitness.

Workout Goals

To complete a 5k race in the fastest possible time.

Workout Duration

The program is based over an intense 6 weeks.

Specific Workout Notes and Guidelines

You should only consider following this program if you enjoy very intensive training and love the feeling of pushing yourself well out of your comfort zone. This program is for very motivated individuals who are totally committed to their cause.

You will require more rest in between demanding workouts. Because of the stresses that these sessions place upon your muscles in particular, you will need to be able to distinguish between simply feeling tired and achy or anything more sinister, such as a slight muscle tear or a pulled ligament, etc.

WEEKS	MONDAY	TUESDAY	WEDNESDAY	THURSDAY	FRIDAY	SATURDAY	SUNDAY
1	Walk/Run 20 minutes	REST	Cross Training 20 minutes	REST	Hill Walk 30 minutes	REST	Run 2 miles
2	Cross Training 35 minutes	REST	Hill Reps 20 minutes	REST	Tempo Run 20 minutes	REST	Timed Run 3 miles
3	Cross Training 40 minutes	REST	Pyramid Training 20 minutes	REST	Run 30 minutes	REST	Tempo Run 2 miles
4	Cross Training 45 minutes	REST	Power Walk 30 minutes	REST	Sprints 30 minutes	REST	Timed Run 3 miles + 1
5	Cross Training 50 minutes	REST	Tempo Run 20 minutes	REST	Run 40 minutes	REST	Tempo Run 3 miles
6	Cross Training 60 minutes	REST	Fartlek Training 30 minutes	REST	Interval Training 40 minutes	REST	Timed Run 3 miles + 1

Hill Walk

Select any hills or inclines nearby to perform this session on. The aim during these workouts is build up strength in the leg muscles and the heart and lungs. You should spend the allotted time actually walking up the hill, so the total time for a session wouldn't include the amount of time you spent walking downhill for example. If you don't have access to any hills, try using an inclinable treadmill or if you aren't able to use one, you can power walk on the flat instead.

Power Walk

You will be brisk walking at a fast pace, maintaining a constant speed. You may start sweating slightly and your breathing should be constantly elevated. A score of 6 or 7/10 on the RPE scale is the perfect level of intensity for you during these walks.

Cross Training

This section of the program is meant to provide aerobic training to improve the strength and endurance of the heart and lungs whilst resting the muscles and joints used during your runs. I suggest swimming, cycling, fitness DVDs, circuit training, etc. Basically, anything which challenges the body differently than running.

Interval Training

You will use three different levels of intensity and speed for these sessions: walking, slow jogging and running. You can either choose to use landmarks for your intervals such as lamp posts or markers in the road or alternatively use a stopwatch to time one-minute intervals at each speed.

Pyramid Training

Choose relatively flat terrain for this session and see section on Pyramid training for further details.

Run

During these runs we ideally want you to be able to maintain a set speed, so don't worry about changing your pace or using different gradients - these types of workouts have their own role in the program. With regards to intensity, you should be aiming for a 7 on the RPE scale. Ideally, I want you to be able to run a set distance, no matter how fast; thereafter you can increase your speeds and improve your running times.

Sunday Sessions

Once a week you will need to develop your endurance by performing some longer runs and building up to race day distance. You can of course choose any day to do this, but to suit the program and fit in with rest days I have structured Sundays as this day.

Hill Reps

Choose the steepest incline you can find within an easy to reach distance from your home. Ideally it should be enough of a challenge that you reach a point where you need to stop running up it because of fatigue in the legs and an unsustainably high breathing rate. If the hill is too steep you will gain the same benefits and improvements by power walking up it.

Following this program, you should be aiming to spend the allotted time actually running or power walking up the hill. Do not include your descent in the overall time you allow for this session. This may well mean running the same section of the hill a number of times which is fine. We are aiming to build in power to the legs and endurance and improve your anaerobic threshold.

Fartlek Training

In phase 4 you will attempt a full 30 minute Fartlek training. For full details see the section in Advanced Training Techniques. Specifically for this session, you are aiming to run the full workout and intersperse this with bursts of faster running or any inclines. You will simply be changing speed when you feel able to. If you feel tired slow down and if you feel fine, increase your speed.

Tempo Run

A tempo run is simply running at a higher speed than you would normally run. These sessions are a little shorter, but the idea is to continue at the increased speed throughout the whole session.

Sprints

You will need to find a flat and dry surface to do these safely and effectively. For more details see section on Advanced Training Techniques.

Timed Run

During this advanced Program 4, we want to get an idea of your race speed and fitness, so you will notice on the Sundays there are 3 timed runs. These should be of race distance, the first one to set a benchmark and subsequent sessions to improve upon. Push yourself hard on these but don't set off too fast and remember to monitor your speed and times.

Timed Mile +

This session is meant to be a monitoring session, where you will time a mile and aim to run at a pace that will allow you to complete the race in your desired time. When you have completed your timed mile, either stop for a few minutes to catch your breath or continue until you complete the desired distance. Timed mile + 2 miles, means you run for a mile whilst timing yourself and then go on to complete a further 2 miles, ideally running.

Preparing for the Race Day

Well, you've managed to get here, hopefully without too many problems or injuries! If your training has gone well you should really be able to fully enjoy the race and possibly run a little faster than usual due to the adrenalin rush and atmosphere.

You have learned the importance of being organized through your training and this is especially important on this day, of all days.

The chances are you will be nervous and have concerns about many things, so don't make your prerace preparation and running kit another worry.

Plan for all types of conditions within reason as the weather can change pretty quickly. Pack all the items you might need and then you can just leave the ones you don't need at the starting line.

Make a list of all the things you wish to take for the race and get them together in the days prior to your departure. Pack your kit bag the night before or before you leave home so you don't forget anything.

Pin your race number on to your top in advance or take some safety pins as spares so you can do it later.

Healthy foods may be very difficult to get hold of on the morning of your race. This is especially important if you have a pre-run meal preference. If possible, take all the food you need with you, because you need to eat something before the race and you don't want to compromise on the quality or type of foods you consume at this time.

A lot of runners take extra layers when they are running in cold conditions and literally discard the clothing halfway through the race when they feel warm enough. Just make sure it's not your favorite or most expensive top, because the chances are you won't get it back!

Your Pre-Race Checklist

ESSENTIALS	POSSIBLES	MEDICAL
Alarm clock	MP3 player	Petroleum jelly (for in
Running shoes	Medical records	between toes, legs etc
2 pairs of running socks	Rainproof jacket	Plasters
Race information	Hat	Muscle rub
Travel itinerary	Gloves	Painkilling gel
Emergency contact list	Running trousers	Antiseptic cream
Running vest or t shirt	Warm up top	Any prescription drugs
Shorts	Towel	Foot powder
Sports bra (ladies only)	Toilet paper	Sun cream
Race confirmation	Sun visor	
details	Sunglasses	
Safety pins	Snack/Pre-race and	
ID tags for your bag	after	
Energy bars	Pedometer	
Energy drinks	Heart rate monitor or	
Bottled water	GPS wrist watch or arm	
	band	

Eating on Race Day

Research has shown that the ideal pre-race meal should be high in carbohydrates with a little low-fat protein to make it more digestible. Here are some ideal options:

- Malt loaf with low fat cheese
- A chicken sandwich (no skin)
- Rice cakes with peanut butter
- Pasta with tuna and a little mayonnaise

Whichever pre-race meal you choose, make sure you have tried it previously, as race day is not the time to experiment with anything new.

A meal that is high in carbohydrates eaten 2 hours prior to running will also help to prevent hypoglycemia (low blood sugar levels). This condition can leave you feeling, tired, dizzy, weak, and unable to finish what you started.

This meal should be at least 1-2 hours before you run to allow sufficient time for digestion and absorption of the foods.

Make sure you drink plenty of fluids up to 1 hour before you start.

Getting any carbohydrates in to your body to replenish glycogen stores during a race can be difficult, although for distances such as a 5k, carbohydrate depletion shouldn't be a problem at all.

Some runners carry small amounts of jellybeans, an energy bar, or a carbohydrate gel to provide an energy boost whilst running. Sipping small amounts of a sports drink regularly can also help you to achieve this.

On Race Day

The key here is to avoid any stress or anxiety so you can focus purely on running the race. Try to stay relaxed and calm, again you can accomplish this by being organized and planning everything well in advance.

Make sure you plan to set your alarm clock much earlier than the time you need to get up. Allow enough time for travelling to the starting line. Plan to be at the starting line at least 1 hour before the start of the race. Drop your belongings off at the designated point allowing you enough time to prepare.

Breakfast

By now you should have a set breakfast or meal that you eat before running. Stick to this today, that is very important. If you are staying in a bed and breakfast or hotel, don't be tempted to get your money's worth and eat a wide array of foods that you wouldn't normally eat before a run.

You should ideally have breakfast about 2 – 3 hours before the start of the race so that the food you have eaten has been sufficiently digested. Eating a larger meal too close to your run could end up leaving you feeling nauseous or getting a stitch when you start to run.

When you are ready to leave, set off leaving plenty of time to spare so that you can get organized properly and take care of any last-minute details.

Before you set off for the race, check the weather forecast one last time for the latest reports, as you may need to wear different clothing. Being aware of the expected weather conditions helps in deciding what you choose to wear for the race.

Use the bathroom before you leave your hotel, B & B, or home.

You should use the journey to the starting line, which you will have already checked out and double checked prior to race day, to focus and mentally prepare for running the race. Try to take deep breaths and relax if you can, and try to stay off your feet as much as possible.

Continue to drink small sips of fluids up to 15 minutes before the start of the race, use the urine test to see if you are sufficiently hydrated – if your urine is clear or very light in color it indicates that you are well hydrated and don't really need any more fluids.

Lining Up for the Start

The rule here is to line up as much as possible according to your fitness level about 15 minutes before the scheduled start time. The faster runners should be at the front. If you don't feel you have a realistic chance of winning the race then you shouldn't be jostling for a place at the front of the lineup.

When slower runners get in front of the faster ones, this can lead to problems. You will be holding up the faster runners, which not only isn't particularly fair on them but also, because of their desire to get in front, can be quite a dangerous situation. In bigger races, people can end up being pushed out of the way, possibly slipping and falling.

Listen to the announcements and try to stay calm. You will feel your heartbeat increase and adrenaline levels rise, so try to keep moving gently but nothing that leaves you feeling tired, just rolling hips, walking on the spot, circling your shoulders, etc. Don't forget to check your shoelaces and if you have been given a race chip make sure it is safely attached to you.

The beginning of any race is usually quite chaotic. When the race starts, don't get caught up in the excitement by yelling and shouting or setting off at a sprint and wasting your energy. Instead, settle yourself down in to a positive state of mind and focus on the job in hand and reaching the finishing line.

Remember to take in the full extent of the atmosphere and the mood of the occasion, as this is usually the part of every race that you remember. As you have been training for this day for the last few weeks, you need to savor every moment.

Running the Race – Race Day Tips

You know that you can complete the distance; you have done so in your training and you are as physically prepared for the race as you can be. If the thought of completing the race in one go is daunting, try visualizing the race in 3 sections of 1 mile each and then mentally tick them off as you pass each point.

Setting the correct pace for your ability level is crucial in a 5k, especially for the first timer. It's very easy to get carried away at the start of the race by going too fast at a pace that you have not prepared for.

The pace that you use during the first mile can sometimes feel almost effortless because of the emotional release and adrenaline rush and excitement of the start of the event. Be careful of setting off too fast because you will really suffer for this later in the race. After the first mile the race will open up; you will have space to run and can settle into your normal pace.

The best idea is to start out a little slower than you are capable of and gradually build up to your usual training speed pace. If you have the strength and endurance left to increase the pace at the latter stages of the race, this can help you get through to the end.

When running any race, it is definitely not a good idea to run the first miles fast in an attempt to get them out of the way. Choosing this strategy will almost certainly mean that you will hit a point where your legs begin to fill with lactic acid and you can no longer maintain that pace and may need to stop.

You will need to be determined and be strong during the latter stages of the race as the will to give up can feel very strong. Don't give into it because you will always live with the thought that you had to walk parts of what might be the only race you ever run.

Keep monitoring your well-being throughout the race and keep adjusting your speed to suit that. Never get bogged down running at a certain pace if it just doesn't feel right for you.

Use your own experience of your longer runs to analyze your ability to keep going at your current pace, but always bear in mind that it is better to try and keep something back in reserve until the end.

The final stages of any race are an incredibly uplifting experience for anybody, with the finishing line meaning so much to so many. Completing the race means a conclusion and an end point to the weeks of training. Many people choose to run for charitable causes and often these pledges of support have kept them going through their lowest points; understandably, these are very emotional times for anyone who is running for the cause of a deceased friend or relative.

For many, crossing the finishing line means the successful realization of a specific goal, an accomplishment that you should be very proud of having achieved.

Life After the Race

Completing a goal that you've worked towards is indeed a great personal accomplishment and you should obviously be very proud about doing so, but on the other hand it can be quite normal for you to feel very low. Whatever your state of mind, it is essential to take care of a few basics prior to relaxing and celebrating.

Recovery from the physical demands of the race should begin as soon as you finish; not following this advice will certainly make your recovery much slower and more painful.

Immediately after the race, treat any blisters or apply some pain-relieving gel to any aching muscles, like your calves or lower back. Don't allow yourself to lie down as this will lead to a number of problems such as cramp or blood pooling, amongst other things.

The time immediately after the race should be used to rehydrate yourself, drinking anything up to 2 liters of water, sports drinks, fruit juices etc.

Take your time to stretch thoroughly within 20 – 30 minutes of finishing the race and multiple times afterwards and over the next few hours.

Alcohol is not a good drink to consume straight after a race, at least not until much later in the day and after you have also had a couple of meals.

If you get the chance to soak your legs in cool water soon after finishing, you will find this very relaxing and therapeutic; later on in the day, have a warm bath to further ease and comfort your aching muscles.

If you can, eat something right after finishing the race, as this will help to increase your blood sugar levels and improve your spirit. If possible, eat a well-balanced meal 2 – 3 hours after the race.

Throughout the day, try to stay slightly active so that you minimize leg muscle soreness and cramping.

One last point: don't forget to go out and celebrate your achievements. You deserve to enjoy your success!

Eating After the Race

As soon as you can after you have completed the race, eat something to replenish your glycogen levels. Current research has shown that the sooner you eat after exercise then the chances of you suffering from muscle fatigue the next day are greatly reduced.

What and when you eat after a race can influence how quickly you recover and how soon you will be able to run again afterwards, so eat a well-balanced meal of which 60% of its content should be carbohydrate based.

The Weeks After Your First Race

After the excitement and euphoria of completing your first 5k, you have a few choices. You'll either want to do another one and run it faster, progress on to a 10k race, or you may well feel that once is enough and you've done your bit. This really depends on how your training went and how easy or challenging you found the race.

If you do decide to run another 5k or move up to the next level and attempt to run a 10k, you need to give yourself a week off from running. Your muscles, bones and joints will benefit from having some time to fully recover, that's not to say you should be totally inactive; instead just try some gentle exercise such as walking or swimming or anything that doesn't place the same stresses on the body as running does. You need to be the judge as to how your body feels and when you think you are ready to resume your training again.

You may well suffer from some muscle soreness after the race, and this could last for a few days before it fully subsides. Regular and gentle stretching will help to speed up the healing and recovery process.

Staying Motivated After the Race

Something that needs to be mentioned here is that one possible after-effect of completing your goal is a feeling of extreme de-motivation. This can be due in part to finally achieving a goal that might have taken a great deal of preparation and effort to actually complete.

Days after the event, some runners can feel a void in their lives as it is the focus of race day that has kept them focused and motivated to keep training. After this has been accomplished, it can often feel like there is nothing to aim for; as a result motivation and enthusiasm can take a serious back step. But hold off on setting new goals until you are mentally and physically ready.

Instead, start running just for fun, don't worry about following a training schedule.

Try some other types of exercise such as cycling, walking, fitness classes etc, or if you feel you need to, take a complete break from running. If it's what you really want to do, the desire to run again will quickly return.

When you have got through this phase, or if you were lucky enough to avoid this period, think about some running goals you'd like to accomplish over the next few months.

Bear in mind that these goals don't have to be centered around running another 5k. You might want to start running faster over the same distance or go a little bit further such as 10k race or perhaps entering a triathlon.

Just allow yourself chance to recover and become passionate about running again before you commit to any more running goals in your own mind.

Final Thoughts

Don't forget: if this is your first 5k we really want you to simply finish the race and not set any world records. If you decide to go on and run further 5k races, those will be the ones to try and improve your times with.

You may well only ever run one 5k, so give it your best shot and aim to run it all, without the need to walk.

Listen, no matter what happens on race day, you should be extremely proud of yourself for getting this far and accomplishing all you have. Think positively, try to enjoy the whole occasion; you have come a long, long way from when you first decided to run a 5k, took the steps to buy this guide, and followed its advice throughout the stages of the training program..

You've got this far, you can do it.

Now all that remains is to go out and run 5k (3.1 miles). I wish you the absolute best of luck. Please write to me to let me know how you get on, that would really mean a lot to me; or leave your feedback in the place you bought this program.

Good luck and thanks for buying and following this running program – Jago

You can contact me here: jago@anewimage.co.uk

About Me

Please allow me to introduce myself. My name is Jago Holmes and I am the author and creator of this 5k training program – "5k Training For Beginners - From Couch To 5K Runner In 8 Weeks Or Less."

I am also the owner and principal trainer here at New Image Personal Training in Halifax, England, one of the North's largest independently owned personal training companies.

We regularly work with over 100 clients each week in our exclusive one-to-one studios.

I am a fully qualified and experienced personal trainer. My company, New Image Personal Training has been in operation for the past 20 years. We consistently get great results from our one-to-one clients and I want to share my knowledge and success with you now.

I have written many newspaper and magazine articles for local press as well as creating a range of digital eBooks and weight loss packages. I regularly present weight loss seminars as well as running my acclaimed "8-week weight loss challenge."

I studied at the University of Leeds, completing my training with YMCA in 2000 after 3 years and attaining the YMCA Personal Trainer award - one of the highest and most respected qualifications available in the UK for Personal Trainers.

As a personal trainer I often work with clients who want to start running seriously and one thing that regularly comes up is a desire to a race.

But one of the biggest problems I find that most runners face is being able to follow and commit the time to using an effective and structured 5k training program.

And this is a real problem, but one that needed fixing so that my clients could take care of their other responsibilities in life like children, work, and family to name but a few and still manage to spend enough time training so they continued to make progress and get fitter.

So, I spent 12 months planning and researching this new program...

- It needed to educate at the same time as being easy to follow.
- It needed to take up minimal time, something which most runners have little of.
- It needed to bring about fast results in the quickest time possible.
- It needed to slot right in to a busy and hectic lifestyle so anyone can do it!

...and I then set about designing this 5k training program, using all the hands-on personal training experience I'd gathered over the years and with the help of a number of clients who were training for or had previously completed 5k races, I tested, refined and improved the system until I finally created the PERFECT solution.

A complete 5k training program which describes in detail exactly how to safely and progressively train for a 5k race in the shortest time physically possible - '5k Training For Beginners - From Couch To 5K Runner In 8 Weeks Or Less'... a simple solution for any runner who wants to run a 5k race whilst avoiding all the potential pitfalls and injury risks associated with running.

Other Books That Might Be of Interest to You

Here are a few more recommended books to help you on your fitness journey. These recipe books will help to keep you energized and feeling wonderful all day. You'll discover loads of delicious recipes which are low in fat, easy to make, and relatively inexpensive to buy the ingredients for. Click on the blue text links below to find out more and discover a wonderful collection of some of the tastiest salad and soups recipes around.

Top Running Tips

Over 100 enlightening and inspiring running tips, strategies, and training techniques that you can use in your own running today.

Fantastic value for money, this book includes dozens of tips that have been put together over a decade of 'in the trenches' running experience both personally and with the help of hundreds of other runners from a wide range of backgrounds and fitness levels. This isn't just another running book full of fluff and filler, inside you'll have access to over 100 genuine performance enhancing techniques and strategies.

http://www.amazon.com/Running-Tips-Ways-Improve-ebook/dp/B00ARJFCH0

Healthy Soups for Healthy Living

Healthy soups are one of the best ways to use a wide range of wholesome fresh meats and vegetables to create amazingly tasty and nutritious meals.

Whether you want a warming soup by the fireside on a cold and frosty winters evening or a refreshingly tangy and delicious midday snack to keep you going through till dinner time in the summer, there's a perfect recipe in this soup cookbook for you.

http://www.amazon.com/Recipes-Quick-Delicious-Healthy-ebook/dp/B009B5GYN2

Healthy Salads for Healthy Living

Preparing your own healthy food often means slaving away for hours, but most of these super quick salads and dressings can be prepared and ready to eat in less than 10 minutes.

Another great thing about making your own salad is it can be a very cheap meal for anyone cooking on a budget.

Salads are no longer simply a summer dish, with the warm salads in this book you can also treat yourself in the middle of winter to a healthy, warming and refreshing meal.

http://www.amazon.com/Healthy-Prepare-Serve-Delicious-ebook/dp/B009FT4PFI

Made in the USA
Middletown, DE
23 December 2022

20315643R00104